The Word-Conscious Classroom

Building the Vocabulary Readers and Writers Need

Judith A. Scott • **Bonnie J. Skobel** • **Jan Wells**

SCHOLASTIC

New York • Toronto • London • Auckland • Sydney
Mexico City • New Delhi • Hong Kong • Buenos Aires

Credits

Our appreciation to the authors and publishers who granted us permission to use the excerpts as follows:

"A Cliché" and "I, Says the Poem." From A SKY FULL OF POEMS by Eve Merriam. Copyright © 1964, 1970, 1973 by Eve Merriam. Reprinted by permission of Marian Reiner.

"Wordhunter's Collection." Copyright © 1985 by Judith Nicholls, from MAGIC MIRROR by Judith Nicholls, published by Faber and Faber. Reprinted by permission of the author.

Various writing rubrics. Copyright © 2004 by Jan Wells and Janine Reid, from WRITING ANCHORS, published by Pembroke. Reprinted by permission.

Cover Photos (from top left): Maria Lilja; Bonnie Jacobs; © Gale Zucker, Sequel Creative via SODA
Cover Design: James Sarfati
Interior Design: LDL Designs
Editor: Gloria Pipkin
Production Editor: Sarah Weaver
Copy Editor: Marla Garfield

ISBN-13: 978-0-439-84566-3
ISBN-10: 0-439-84566-1

To our families, who supported us

To our friends, who encouraged us

*To teachers everywhere, who continue to inspire us with their
dedication and commitment*

But most important, to our students, who adopted these ideas and soared

——✳——

Contents

Acknowledgments

T his book is the culmination of many years of working together. It sat, bubbling beneath the surface of our busy lives, for a very long time. Over the years, so many people contributed ideas and inspiration for the book that it is hard to know where to begin. We are grateful for all our colleagues who listened to us, asked questions, shared their stories, and tried these ideas in their classrooms. We learned so much from you. We are grateful to our students, and students everywhere, who learned to embrace the role of writers and critical readers. We are awed by what you can do when given the freedom and power to do it. And we are particularly indebted to Teresa Blackstone, Susie Cross, and Alan Jones, the other core teacher-researchers in our vocabulary group. Their thoughts and ideas are woven tightly with ours.

Our work on this project exists because of the generous funding of the Canadian government through the Social Sciences and Humanities Research Council of Canada (grant #410-92-1654 and #31-639143) , and continues to grow through sponsorship by the United States government's National Center for Education Research and the Vocabulary Innovations in Education (VINE) project (IES grant #R305G060140). Invaluable research assistance and support came from Cindy Butler, Sarah Henry Gallant, Marlene Asselin, and Dianne Jamieson-Noel.

Others, too, deserve special mention. Bill Nagy provided inspiration to the group. The LOMCIRA gang, Janine Reid, the M.A. students from Simon Fraser, the B.C. Early Literacy and Later Literacy Network, Pat Holborn, Yrsa Jensen, and many other instructional leaders from the Lower Mainland contributed to our thinking and encouraged us in innumerable ways. We also acknowledge Susan Close (1988) for coining the Gifts of Words phrase and Ted Hayes for bringing this idea, and the thought-provoking writing from his students, to our attention.

Many teachers have adapted these ideas, and Donna Scott and Tatiana Miller deserve particular acknowledgment for inviting us to use their classroom extensions in Chapters 7 and 11. Donna also helped by responding to drafts of the book on her summer holiday. What a good sister! In addition, the book would not look the same without the artistic contributions of Nate, Rainie, Jennie, Rosie, Molly, and Emily. Thank you all!

Heartfelt thanks go to each and every student we've ever taught, particularly the ones in our classes and schools between 1991 and 2007. Students in Surrey School District No. 36, particularly those at Coyote Creek and Cindrich elementary schools, and children in Vancouver School District No. 39, especially those at Dr. R. E. McKechnie Elementary school, gave us much of the incentive, substance, and insight for this book. We hope you are continuing to write well.

The editorial staff at Scholastic has been phenomenal in encouraging, supporting, and editing this manuscript. Special thanks go out to Margery Rosnick, Gloria Pipkin, Sarah Weaver, Marla Garfield, Ray Coutu, and Terry Cooper.

Living the "writerly life" is not easy. How grateful we are for our fabulous families. Our husbands, children, parents, and siblings provided graceful encouragement and humor that buoyed us as we created this document. In particular, our partners—John Sheibley, Frank Skobel, and Jerry George—have been incredible bastions of support and love.

—— ❈ ——

Introduction

This book is about developing a word-conscious classroom, where teachers and students are excited by words and appreciate the power of words as tools for communication. When you think about word learning, you may sigh and think of vocabulary booklets where students memorize lists of unrelated words in order to pass a test. Let us assure you—this is not how we conceptualize vocabulary learning, although, to be honest, it's not far from how some of us started. The purpose of this book is to take you on our journey as teachers and researchers who came together to try to improve vocabulary instruction in classrooms. We want to help you infuse vocabulary learning in your classroom throughout each and every day. We have found that creating such a word-conscious classroom can make a tremendous difference in your students' abilities to write interesting stories and other text types, read critically, and join in the literary discourse of schools.

When we talk about vocabulary learning, we are talking about both concept development and understanding the meaning of words. Other aspects of word learning, such as spelling and decoding, are related and important, but we are choosing to focus on developing word meanings within an integrated approach to language development. This means understanding new words in both oral and written language as well as expanding the ability to use words, to understand multiple meanings for the same word, to understand the nuances of using a word, and to understand how a word fits into a larger schema of understanding. As we build vocabulary knowledge, we are building both world knowledge and knowledge of how words work in the English language (Hirsch, 2003).

When Bonnie asked her sixth-grade class to describe the most important thing they'd learned as writers from spending a year in her class, Abhidi said, "Before, when we did writing, we just did stories. Putting powerful language, like metaphors, similes, or changing *said* to *yelled* makes my stories more powerful. I never knew that would make my story better before, but it makes my stories more powerful and people like to read them."

In this book, we take the position that learning about words is as central as breathing in a literacy classroom, because words are the cornerstone of both oral and written language. Learning about words is inseparable from learning about reading and learning about writing. And, when they are taught together, a synchrony exists that goes beyond all three.

Come Along for the Ride

In this book, we invite you join us on a whirlwind ride through ten years of laughing, playing, working, and learning together. We think it's important for you to realize how these ideas came together and to know that they have been refined through experiences with real students in real classrooms. The ideas in this book come, for the most part, out of our explorations together as we tried to integrate what we know about good literacy practices with what we know about vocabulary learning. A group of us, including the three authors, were part of a teacher research project with a focus on vocabulary that met for dinners, discussion, and brainstorming sessions for almost a decade. These meetings were part of what we call a think tank model of professional development and exploration (Henry et al., 1999). In this model, teachers and researchers come together, each bringing a high level of expertise in his or her own area. The combined expertise in our meeting room was amazing.

Bonnie had taught for 30 years, served as the social studies helping teacher for her district, and, as a faculty associate (on loan from her district to supervise student teachers), taught the language arts methodology course for Simon Fraser University. At the time of this project, Bonnie was both a grade 6/7 teacher and the principal of an urban elementary school where students came from a variety of cultures and spoke several different languages.

Jan had been a teacher for 23 years, the reading consultant for a large urban metropolitan district in Ontario, and a faculty associate who taught both the reading and the language arts methodology courses for Simon Fraser University. She was a grade 4/5 teacher at the time of the project and later became the primary literacy consultant for the Vancouver School Board. Both Bonnie and Jan had taught several different grades, from primary to intermediate, throughout their careers.

Judy was an assistant and later associate professor in reading and literacy at Simon Fraser University after finishing her dissertation in educational psychology/curriculum and instruction/reading/vocabulary at the University of Illinois at Urbana-Champaign. Prior to that she had been a teacher and graduated with a Reading Specialist credential from the University of California at Davis.

Other core members of the group mentioned throughout the book were a band of exemplary classroom teachers: Teresa Blackstone, Alan Jones, and Susie Cross. Cindy Butler was the main behind-the-scenes research assistant for the project, and she entered the teaching profession during this project.

Our common connection came through Simon Fraser University, where several members of the group had served as faculty associates, took classes, or taught classes on literacy. From the outset, it was clear that the members of the vocabulary group shared a common vision and theoretical frame. In particular, we were informed by Lev Vygotsky's notion of sociocultural interactions and the power of discussion as a means to create new understandings and expand our horizons (Vygotsky, 1978).

When Judy received a grant to explore alternatives to traditional vocabulary instruction, she invited members of the group to join her as teacher researchers who combined their expertise in teaching with her knowledge of vocabulary research. The diversity of perspectives was celebrated as essential in their construction of new understandings about effective vocabulary instruction. Coming together as a group of experts alleviated many of the issues associated with collaborative projects, such as hierarchy, credibility, and ownership (Henry et al., 1999). Because their expertise as teachers brought them to the group, the teachers didn't feel as though they were unequal partners. Instead, their expertise was explicitly valued and encouraged to flourish. The university participants were also acknowledged as experts in the research community who could offer a different set of skills and abilities to the group. Our unique strengths contributed to our abilities to learn from each other, help each other, reflect on our practices, engage in shared critique of those practices, and support one another in making professional choices and change. In one paper written about this project, we identified these elements of the group dynamic as essential in contributing to the sense of community: (a) safety, built on respect, (b) engaging dialogue, (c) collaboration among equals, (d) personal commitment, and (e) time.

The topic, vocabulary learning, was defined, but how we explored it together and what we produced were not. The teacher researchers and university researchers all acknowledge that they changed and benefited from their involvement in the project (Henry et al., 1999). We were all energized by the opportunity to discuss ideas, practice, and problems with each other.

After Bonnie gave a workshop for a local school, the principal, Grant McIntosh, thanked her by presenting her with this story:

She was arriving at school feeling bored and listless. The spectre of another morning reading her students' stories, dripping with mindless violence and populated by mundane characters, was daunting. She needed a teaching makeover desperately! She yearned to hear real children's voices in their writing, real emotion, real people, the imagination that kids have. Where could she go? It wasn't as if there was a shop like a beauty salon where one can go for this kind of service. Mud mask? Hair color? Nails? Style? Massage? New way of teaching writing?

Just when her life was at its darkest, when she was considering a career in real estate, she got a call that was to change her life—well, her teaching life, anyway. She joined a group of teachers who shared some of the same feelings about kids' writing. They talked about it, they laughed, they cried, and they looked for ways to help children tap into their rich imaginations. She brought real stories with powerful language to the students and let them borrow and steal words and characters and ideas for their writing. She developed all kinds of strategies to help kids discover, enjoy, and play with language. They wrote poems, memories, adventure stories, and picture books. They wrote like readers and read like writers! It was like a renaissance in her classroom . . . (fast-forward three years).

Now every day she rushes to school, flushed with excitement at the prospect of reading her children's stories and seeing the fruits of her labors. Right? Get real! But at least now there is a possibility that she will be able to read some writing that is fresh, interesting, dynamic, imaginative. She'll settle for just one of these. (Skobel, 1998)

This humorous essay shows why we did what we did. In the workshop, Bonnie conveyed her previous sense of despair as a teacher of writing and the excitement she felt as her students began to become conscious of the power of words as tools of communication. Many teachers share her struggle. Perhaps you are one of them. If so, we hope our explanations of struggles and successes will enable you to ponder your own practice and help you with the vital job of teaching students to be better readers, writers, and word users.

How the Book Is Organized

This approach to vocabulary learning may sound daunting. Please realize that the purpose of this book is to strip away some of the anxiety that teachers may feel when they think about teaching vocabulary. In this book you will find practical activities tried by classroom teachers who were exploring how to use what we know about teaching and learning to inform the teaching and learning of vocabulary. In the process, we developed techniques that helped students become both more expressive writers and more critical readers. Adding to a teacher's workload is certainly not our intent. The teachers we know and work with are all juggling the various demands of classroom life with skill and dedication. We hope that this book conveys our enjoyment in discovering ways to infuse this approach into the everyday working environment of the classroom.

The rest of this book is about how to create an enticing vocabulary-learning environment for children, a place where word learning is woven into the daily fabric of reading, writing, speaking, and listening. It is based on both theory and actual experiences with children and classrooms. In the first chapter, we introduce the concept of word consciousness and our general theoretical frame. In Chapter 2, we expand on the idea that authors give readers a gift—the eloquence of their words. In Chapter 3, the goal is to raise general awareness and interest in words through games and other stand-alone activities. Infusing word consciousness into classrooms can take place on many levels, and this chapter introduces methods to generate excitement about words as well as increase the volume of vocabulary exposure. Chapters 4 and 5 discuss the use of cherished books, touchstone books, and mentor texts to scaffold word awareness, starting with whole-class modeling and facilitation, and moving toward word consciousness in independent reading. Looking carefully at mentor texts allows a student to develop a bank of words. Then, in Chapters 6 through 10, we demonstrate how to encourage students to draw on this bank of words in their own writing. Again, we start with whole-class modeling and facilitation and move toward word consciousness in independent writing.

The teacher is the guide in this explicit development of word consciousness. However, the role of the teacher is that of a facilitator, a coach, a leader, and a collaborator. It is through focused discussion, scaffolded interactions, and experimentation that students develop and create ownership over the words they encounter and use in schools. It is also through these sorts of experiences that children learn about the power of language in our classrooms.

In Chapter 11, we turn our attention to assessment and evaluation. Although this topic is addressed at the end of the book, it is not the case that evaluation is considered last in our planning. In fact, establishing criteria for success—developing rubrics and rating scales together with our students—is an important part of teaching. When we show the criteria for success, the learner becomes involved in the ongoing assessment of his or her own learning. The last chapter revisits our theoretical frame and emphasizes the next steps in developing a word-conscious classroom, given the content of the book.

The shared vision outlined in this introduction provides the foundation, as does our conviction that classrooms are best conceived of as communities of children, all of whom are active constructors of meaning, operating on multiple levels of negotiated tasks toward clearly specified outcomes.

—— ✳ ——

Chapter 1

Developing a Word-Conscious Classroom

Y ou can enjoy a piece of art or music because of the pleasure it brings to you. However, if you have taken an art appreciation class or a music appreciation class, your depth of understanding is increased and your level of appreciation is raised. The development of word consciousness is the development of the appreciation of how words work to convey images and thoughts combined with an interest in, and awareness about, the structure and power of words (Anderson & Nagy, 1992; Graves & Watts-Taffe, 2002; Scott & Nagy, 2004). Paying attention to the way writers use words is analogous to becoming conscious of how chords blend together to create music.

Word Consciousness: What Is It?

Word consciousness can be thought of as the metacognitive or metalinguistic knowledge that a learner brings to the task of word learning. Native speakers possess implicit knowledge about the way their language works (Bloom, 2000; Nagy & Scott, 2000). Just as a musician can recognize when music is off-key, so native speakers can recognize when word use or syntax is unusual. Word consciousness also allows a depth of understanding that can help students acquire not just specific words but also a facility to learn words in general (Scott & Nagy, 2004). This knowledge is generative. That is, it consists of knowledge and dispositions that transfer to, and enhance, students' learning of other words beyond that particular topic or that particular word.

Words are not isolated units. They are multidimensional, with connections to other sets of both semantic and linguistic knowledge (Nagy & Scott, 2000; Cummins, 2000). Think, for instance, of everything you know about the word *erupt*. You may know that it is related morphologically to other words like *eruption*, *erupted*, and *rupture*. You may also have thought about the types of things that can erupt: *volcanoes*, *people*, *geysers*, *boils*, or *pimples*. Or, your thoughts may have turned to what emerges during an eruption: *lava*, *anger*, *steam*, or *pus*. All this knowledge is linked in your mind, along with an understanding of what sort of scenario might include the word *erupt* and other words that might appear with it (e.g., *mountain*, *cinder*, *ashes*). The more times you encounter a word, the more information you build up as a word schema for that concept (Nagy & Scott, 2000; Stahl, 2003).

In order to develop a sense of metacognitive control over word learning, students need to focus on words themselves as well as on how to learn words and how to use words well. In order to develop conscious control over where to place their fingers on a piano, or ways to enhance the timing of the piece, music students usually begin by listening to, and playing, pieces of music written by another composer. This is a commonly accepted practice before students compose their own music. We use this analogy purposefully, because writing is like composing a piece of music. Yet we often do not give students the time or the explicit mediated assistance they need to understand and use words in their own written work as effectively as published authors do. Authors give us "Gifts of Words," wonderfully composed phrases that capture the essence of what they want to say. We ask our students to find these Gifts of Words in the books we read aloud or on our own. Then, part of our instruction involves clarifying how authors use these gifts to create powerful images. We've found that this modeling of word choice by published authors and discussions about conscious word choice help students gain control over words they use in their own writing.

Bakhtin (1981) claimed that learning words involves learning how others have used words, saying that every word is half someone else's. Gaining control over word learning happens when speakers and writers use the word, adapting it to their own semantic and expressive intent. This notion, called ventriloquism, assumes that any use of the word contains both the voice of the current speaker and the voices of those who have used the same word, or pattern of discourse, within the context in which the word, or pattern of discourse, was learned. In order to become "owners" of words (or patterns of discourse), learners need to actively appropriate, or take as their own, these new forms of speaking and writing (Wertsch, Tulviste, & Hagstrom, 1993).

The development of conscious control over language use and the ability to negotiate the social and academic language of schooling are particularly important for students who do not generally fare well in schools. Differences in the type of language structures, interaction styles, and vocabulary found in many homes mean that the language of schooling is significantly different from the language many students encounter prior to entering school (Heath, 1983; Zentella, 1997). The language of books, particularly books found inside schools, may contain a high proportion of words that are rarely encountered outside of school (Chafe & Danielewicz, 1987; Cummins, 2000).

English is an interesting language because only about 100 words make up 50 percent of all the words we use in writing (Carroll, Davies, & Richman, 1971). These words, such as *is*, *the*, *and*, *or*, and *but*, are the glue that holds English together. Beyond these, there is a core set of frequently used words that almost all native English speakers would consider well known. These are words that occur often in both oral and written language, such as *ball*, *mother*, and *house*. It is estimated that we use approximately 5,000 different words to communicate ideas when we speak. However, there are approximately 300,000 different root words in the English language. The 295,000 extra words are the ones that add richness and texture to our language. They are also more precise words that can be used to communicate nuances, such as the difference between *stare* and *glance*, as well as technical terms such as *stethoscope*. Being able to communicate in an academic genre requires the understanding and use of these more precise words. Developing a word-conscious classroom is a way to provide students with activities and a type of apprenticeship that can guide the purposeful development of academic discourse.

For many students, the language of textbooks and novels constitutes a new social language. Children need a chance to learn how to appropriate such language and make it their own. Traditionally, the teaching and learning of words has taken place in schools during reading instruction, where knowledge of individual word meanings is most commonly taught prior to reading a story. Alternatively, specific vocabulary words have been taught as they relate to content areas. The goal of much of this instruction has been to promote the development of discrete word meanings (Blachowicz, 1987). This is an admirable goal, but it doesn't go far enough in challenging the academic gap that exists between groups of advantaged and disadvantaged students (Chall, Jacobs, & Baldwin, 1990; Hart & Risley, 1995; 2003). This book describes how teachers can strategically mentor the development of students' appreciation for words, as well as focus on understanding individual word meanings and patterns of discourse. This type of knowledge is critical when students are learning a new social language with words and patterns of discourse that do not mirror the words and patterns of language used on a daily basis outside of school. Students need to form the knowledge and attitude toward language that will help them develop dispositions toward words beyond the individual lessons taught.

Instructional Scaffolding and Situated Learning

Instructional scaffolding is the heart and soul of our approach. A sociocultural perspective (Vygotsky, 1978) and the idea of legitimate peripheral participation (Lave & Wenger, 1991) both inform our practice. With instructional scaffolding, the teacher sets up learning situations in which students are working at an appropriate level to gain independence in their ability to perform a task. During the learning process, the teacher engages in constructive dialogue, shares responsibility for the learning that is taking place, and gradually releases responsibility until the student is able to perform the task independently (Pearson & Gallagher, 1983). As learning occurs, the students move through their zone of proximal development (ZPD), which is defined as the difference between what a child can do independently and the potential steps the child can achieve with adult guidance or with the guidance of more capable peers (Vygotsky, 1978; Tharp & Gallimore, 1989). The emphasis is on teachers and students working together in joint productive activity, grounded in authentic experiences, with a goal of student success rather than evaluation.

Think back to when you learned to ride a bicycle or to a time when you helped a child learn this skill. First of all, there was probably a desire to graduate from a tricycle to a bicycle. This usually occurs with adult assistance, although at this point the adult does not yet know how this whole process will unfold or the length of time it will take. Most likely, the progression and transfer of responsibility occurred as a move to training wheels, followed by an adult's holding, with great force, the seat of the bike and running alongside the child. This might have progressed to a light hold on the seat, to not holding at all but still running beside the rider, to stopping and letting the rider realize her success. Finally, the rider proceeds to doing wheelies in the driveway completely unassisted. The whole time this process is happening there is dialogue between the rider and the adult with encouragement and guidance about how to do the task.

Learning to ride a bike happens individually for each rider, depending on her prior knowledge and experiences, within her ZPD. How that knowledge or skill is acquired depends on the kind of interaction and collaboration that occurs between the rider and the adult. Using the above analogy, the adult may take the beginning bike rider to a grassy flat field where falls won't be as traumatic, moving to the top of a slight incline as the rider's confidence improves. She might also ensure that it is a relatively empty area and, as she holds the bike, offer the appropriate amount of support. With scaffolding, the original support is gradually removed, leaving students as stronger and more independent learners. This involves the constant adjustment of the amount of adult intervention to the child's developing needs and abilities. Just as the adult teaching a child to ride a bike provides an appropriate level of support that changes with the child's expertise, so does the teacher provide a level of support that changes as a learner's expertise grows. The transfer of responsibility is facilitated by talk. The adult might tell the rider to pedal faster, turn the handlebars, or brake. This talk is meaningful—it is directed at eventual success and helps the learner focus on essential components of the activity. Productive conversations often allow learners to discuss strategies and ideas with each other as well as the teacher.

In the bike-riding analogy, the rider and her immediate needs determine the next tidbit of advice. When to teach how to turn or stop the bike depends on the individual and the circumstances. In addition, adults teach their children how to ride bikes when there is motivation to do so, and the children usually have a say in the direction of their learning. The adult and child are partners who share the responsibility for learning as the adult gives warm and encouraging feedback on strategies the child is using. We don't know of any parent who hands a 5-year-old a learn-to-ride manual and then sits back and observes!

Linking Word Consciousness to Your Curriculum

You may feel that you already have so much to think about in your classroom that a focus on vocabulary might be too much. Why bother? We've discovered three answers to this question.

First, reading the writing of others shows us how powerful words can be when used in exciting and unusual ways, ways we would never think of in everyday speech. Everyday conversational words are limited in scope. We learn about "writerly" ways of saying things by reading the work of published writers. The type of language found in books is quite different from the language found in everyday conversations. Children's books contain almost twice as many sophisticated words as conversations among college graduates (Hayes & Ahrens, 1988). However, an awareness of words, a love of words, and a curiosity about words don't just develop by themselves. Students who can recognize powerful language and use it themselves in their writing have developed this awareness through scaffolding by adults in their lives. Not all children have equal access to this sort of scaffolding for English vocabulary from parents, particularly if parents speak a different language. Vocabulary knowledge builds up over time and, as teachers, we need to provide opportunity and access to sophisticated language so that all children can become aware of the power of words, and develop an awareness and curiosity about words that will facilitate their academic careers.

Second, we learn to make sense of unknown words, and we add them to our lexicon through exposure to these words in both reading and discussion. The original author of the Hardy Boys series, Leslie MacFarlane, supposedly said that he deliberately inserted the odd "jaw-breaker" into his stories, words that would challenge his readers to think. He believed in writing "up" to his readers, not down. Older readers who remember reading the Hardy Boys may recall the density of the text—yet we were hooked. The stories drove us on regardless of the vocabulary. When we came to a hard word, as long as it didn't stop the flow of the story, we read on.

Similarly, very young children listen to the stories of Beatrix Potter. They hear about Peter Rabbit, who, when caught in the gooseberry net by his brass buttons, "gave himself up for lost" but was "implored to exert himself" (p. 33) by the friendly sparrows. While the precise meaning of the words is beyond the 3-year-old listener, the feeling of the words and the emotion of the moment are caught in the power of the language and the contextual clues of story and pictures. This is important because words are learned incrementally over time. The first time you are exposed to a word, you may put it into a general context (in this case, something that might happen in a garden). As you are exposed to it again and again, you figure out a bit more each time (he was caught by some type of net; a gooseberry might be like a strawberry or a raspberry).

Much of the vocabulary students learn before they arrive in school is learned in context—that is, while doing something and talking about it. They acquire new words because those words match the concepts being discussed. This continues throughout the first years of school. And it works equally well with older students. The act of reading aloud brings different settings and times into the classroom, times and places that students visit vicariously. Oral discussions about read-aloud books are an excellent way to build vocabulary growth. While we advocate continuing read-alouds into the upper grades, as students get older, another context for learning new words, independent reading, comes into play. Students read in all subject areas, so they read science, social studies, and math texts in addition to chapter books. They are given articles and extracts to read, and they most often read these on their own.

Becoming a prolific reader creates a situation where a child is exposed to a great many words and becomes able to build vocabulary knowledge as she sees the words repeatedly. Although not all students in your class will be prolific readers, the concept of scaffolding word learning through wide reading—the reading of many different books—means that we ask all students to read texts that are sufficiently challenging regarding new and unknown words. There is a fine balance here because a text too dense with new words will frustrate readers. A masterful teacher is aware of the child's ability to handle new texts (books within the appropriate ZPD) and uses this knowledge when matching books with readers. This point is another reason why reading aloud to students at all levels is such a valuable use of instructional time. When we read aloud, we are exposing students to a wider vocabulary than many of them can read on their own, and providing the opportunity for them to gain incremental word knowledge.

As students read at more mature levels, the problem-solving work of figuring out meanings from context and using aspects of their current vocabulary knowledge to work out what a new word might mean becomes increasingly important. For example, a student reading about the biosphere, who already understands the meaning of *bio* from other words like *biology* and *biography*, may pay attention to references to the atmosphere and the stratosphere in her science text and deduce that *biosphere* has something to do with the area around the earth that can sustain life forms.

How many of our students can bring these sophisticated powers of deduction and inference to their daily reading? How many of them will want to? It is easier and quicker to "skip over" the hard words and get the general gist of a piece, especially if it is an exciting story. The general overall meaning is often quite sufficient for anyone to be able to engage in a whole-class discussion, answer a few questions, and appear to be fully informed. Unfortunately, the unknown words remain unknown and the students' overall word knowledge is increased only slightly. Their understanding of the morphology and interrelated network of origin and usage that connects words in the English language is not developed, and in an increasingly detrimental fashion, their ability to decode and comprehend academic language is affected. Creating a focus on the language used by authors creates motivation to closely examine word use.

A third reason to focus on words is that it provides students with the means for more accurate communication with others. Most children want their writing to sound sophisticated but are often frustrated by their communication through writing. Learning how to write well is equivalent to learning any other skill. Sometimes it's useful to imitate the work of more skilled writers until you are able to find your own voice. These models and explanations can provide the framework for expression and can give students the confidence to both experiment and use language effectively to convey their ideas. According to Butler (2002), imitation allows students to see models of successful writing and gives them a chance to work with the text, manipulate models, and transform them in meaningful ways.

Shared Vision and Theoretical Frame

Schools often write vision statements or try to articulate what elements of practice are important for daily interactions with students. We didn't sit down together and develop the framework that follows, but it captures the collective understanding of the group about teaching and learning that emerged as we worked together. In particular, these statements reflect our knowledge and understanding of pedagogy that inform our teaching of vocabulary. These themes and understandings are woven into the fabric of our teaching, and you will see them manifested in many different contexts throughout the book:

- Students learn when they are working and talking with others.
- Students learn when the work is neither too hard nor too easy.
- Students need teachers to help them learn.
- Students need to learn not only words, but *about* words.

- Students learn about words by paying attention to published authors.
- Students can learn to be strategic about word learning and word use.
- Students can learn to take responsibility for their own learning.
- Students learn best when they are engaged and interested.
- Student are more engaged when they work on authentic tasks of their own choosing.
- Students learn best in a safe, warm, and fun environment.

We hope these statements help you understand our particular stance toward teaching and learning. One of the tensions in our group was the lack of connection between what we knew to be good classroom practice and the materials available for teaching vocabulary. One of the reasons for writing this book is to share how we were able to meld vocabulary learning with the set of beliefs and understandings set out in this first chapter. In particular, we realized that the development of word consciousness could be a powerful tool for vocabulary learning that honored and expanded our collective understanding of important conditions for learning. This book blends knowledge of vocabulary learning and classroom practice so that students can read, use, and recognize words as tools of communication.

Backward Planning

Wiggins and McTighe (1998) discuss the importance of understanding the end goals of your instruction and working backward from these goals to the components that need to be in place to achieve them. As a group, we knew what we wanted as end goals. We wanted students who were critical, thoughtful readers and powerful writers who could express their thoughts and ideas well—or at least better than we'd been able to get students to read and write in the past. We also liked the idea of seeing our students interested in and excited by words, with tools to unlock the meanings of new words. However, the goal of word consciousness and vocabulary development was really secondary to the development of our students' overall literacy. We see vocabulary development as one way to facilitate their reading and writing in general. Our challenge was figuring out how to get there.

As we look back on what we did, we can capture it in the following:

- We increased the volume of exposure to sophisticated language in our classrooms.
- We established classroom communities where it was considered normal to ask about

word meanings, experiment with language use, and to have not only the teacher, but other students, serve as vocabulary coaches.

- We used our knowledge of what worked in teaching and learning in other arenas to develop activities where the student needed to pay attention to words in order to "play the game."
- We fostered communities that nurtured appreciation of word use and developed consciousness about words as tools of communication.

——— ✳ ———

Chapter 2

Building a Bank of Powerful Language

How to Get Started

This poem by Judith Nicholls (1985) helps introduce the concept of word consciousness both to you as a reader and to your students at the beginning of the year.

Wordhunter's Collection

By Judith Nicholls

There's wiggle and giggle
Goggles and swatch,
Straggle and gaggle
And toggle and itch.

Glimmering, shimmering,
Glistening, twinkle,
Poppycock, puddle
And muddle and pimple.

Peapod and flip-flop,
Rickety, dodo,
Murmuring, lingering,
Galaxy, yo-yo.

Extra terrestrial's
One that I love,
Betelgeuse, Pluto—
Heavens above!

Who would not fall
For a bird called a chickadee?
A widgeon or warthog
Or just the old chimpanzee?

Many's the word
That I capture each day,
Whispering each
Till I know it will stay.

Raising Word Consciousness

Reading, writing, and collecting words begin the day our students enter the classroom. Before we meet the class, we collect numerous well-written novels and picture books at a variety of reading levels and display them attractively in the classroom. (See the bibliography for a list of suggested books.) These books contain poetic prose, vivid descriptions of setting or character, and examples of word use that we want to highlight throughout the year. In other words, these books provide the raw material for word learning in our classrooms. Reading and writing are reciprocal acts, with each informing the other. Our stance is that students grow tremendously in their feel for, and use of, language when they are immersed in rich literature, in an environment with ample opportunities to write, and with the supportive mediation of a teacher.

When your program is enhanced by word consciousness, it is infused with an enthusiasm for vocabulary that will make looking at words compelling and fascinating. Once your students have become readers who wear the lenses of word hunters, they will never again skip over those "jaw-breakers" or pass over a simile without a smile of recognition. Instead, they become avid searchers for the best and most powerful words. Hearing language read aloud and discussing the language used by authors are the cornerstones of the word-conscious classroom. We read from a wide variety of materials and use this time to model and think aloud about reading strategies as well as the content of the material. We explore genres and ways in which authors construct their messages. Books and authors are our teachers. This practice forms a bridge into the writing program, providing models and scaffolds for apprentice writers to build upon. We try to read like writers, bearing in mind William Faulkner's exhortation, "Read, read, read. Read everything—trash, classics, good and bad, and see how they do it. Just like a carpenter who works as an apprentice and studies the master. Read! You'll absorb it. Then write. If it is good, you'll find out. If it's not, throw it out the window" (Faulkner, 1968, p. 55).

In the course of reading aloud, we are teaching elements of style and voice that are unfamiliar to our students. At the beginning of our project, students were asked how they could improve their writing. Their answers usually focused on punctuation ("I need to learn how to use commas") or spelling ("I would be a better writer if I was better at spelling. I need to study harder"). By the end of the year they were making statements like these: "You need to read books on stuff you want to write about" (Soleste, grade 6); "Think a lot and spend time on things; believe your story can be good and not quit in the middle" (Rob, grade 6); "Learn how to write so the reader has pictures in their mind" (Maria, grade 5); and "Learn to express your feelings with powerful language" (Emma, grade 6).

During the course of the year, we taught our students systematically to look at language, to look at ways in which writers use language, and to examine effective devices such as metaphor, simile, alliteration, strong verbs, and powerful adjectives. We consistently asked them to look at the work of writers through new lenses and to learn from the masters.

Study a wide variety of literature!

Like playing pieces of music written by another composer before composing your own music, the explicit purpose of this mediated assistance is to help students get a feel for the way exemplary authors use language in books. Rather than teach a discrete set of words, we help students become aware of word choice and place value on their attempts to imitate mentor texts in their own writing.

Building the Word Bank

To initiate this process of looking at authors' word choices, we explain that authors, like painters, try to create an image for their audience: a painter with paints, an author with words. Then we begin collecting the words and phrases we find in books and poems that we find enticing. We model the process in whole-group discussions, by stopping during read-alouds and pointing out similes, metaphors, strong verbs, precise nouns, or unusual juxtapositions of words that the author used to develop a picture in the minds of the readers. As mentioned in the previous chapter, we call these "Gifts of Words." The word *gift* implies something special—in this case, a gift of exquisite language to build powerful images.

Picture books, poems, and novels are all used as texts for student learning. For instance, Jan, as she reads *Mrs. Frisby and the Rats of NIMH*, stops at the description of the entrance of the rats' hole under the rosebush and says: "Listen to what I just read. Robert O'Brien says that the rats' hole is 'concealed and protected by dense tangles of fiercely sharp thorns.' What a great image! You know how your hair gets tangled in knots sometimes when you sleep? When I read this, I think about those tangles having sharp thorns and how hard it would be to get through that. That seems like really good protection for a rat hole. I doubt many other animals would want to get down in there. And the thorns are 'fiercely sharp.' What else can we think of that might be 'fiercely sharp'?"

In this way, phrases, such as *fiercely sharp*, are gathered along with other words, phrases, and sentences to form a Bank of Powerful Language. This bank serves as a repository for strong vocabulary that the authors in our classes can visit in the future, when they wish to withdraw such words and phrases for their own writing (see Figure 2-1).

Usually, there are several sorts of read-alouds during the course of a day. A picture book is often used in the morning to introduce the writing workshop; a nonfiction title may be read aloud in science class; poetry and a novel may be shared at another time. These novels read aloud begin the process of building a classroom community. There is a shared common experience that members can refer back to throughout the day and the year. As the class gathers for the daily session with a good book, there is also a sense of belonging and excitement. Titles such as *I Am*

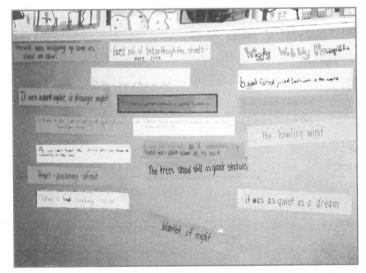

Fig. 2-1: Bulletin Board Showing a Bank of Powerful Language

David, by Anne Holm; *The Giver*, by Lois Lowry; *Hoot*, by Carl Hiaasen; and *Holes*, by Louis Sachar are just a few that have been enjoyed in our classrooms.

When the students become familiar with the concept of gathering Gifts of Words, they begin to identify them during the read-aloud sessions. The following Gifts of Words were chosen by students after reading the first chapter of *The Half-a-Moon Inn* by Paul Fleischman:

- *A chill darted up his spine.*
- *He felt as restless as a chipmunk.*
- *He burst out of bed as though the sheets were afire.*

As the year progresses, the teachers and students have overlapping roles: the teachers continue to provide models of good writing by introducing good children's authors to the class, and the students begin to take a more active role by sharing the Gifts of Words they have discovered in their individual and small-group reading. Together, both students and teachers explore literary devices and language use by authors. These literary devices are explored more fully in Chapters 4 and 5. The attention given to word choice by experienced authors is a vehicle to make students conscious of the discourse of literary writing.

As they sit in a circle, the students share their Gifts of Words. Juan shares a passage from a new book by Erin Hunter: "When he raised his head feebly he saw a waterfall thundering down into the pool in a whirl of foam and spray" (*Moonrise*, p. 90). Tara found, "Something gnawed at his mind, like a mouse at the corner of a rice basket" (K. Paterson, *Rebels of the Heavenly Kingdom*, p. 40). These phrases or sentences are then added to the bank.

TALKING ABOUT WORD CHOICE

Meaningful dialogue about words, style, and the author's meaning or intent is a critical part of developing student understanding. The poem at the beginning of this chapter, "Wordhunter's Collection," can be used to focus that dialogue.

Copy the poem onto an overhead transparency and give students individual copies. Read the poem aloud once, read it twice, and read it chorally with the class. Have your students talk about this poem in pairs and then in small groups, using the following questions as prompts:

- What words did you like? Not like?
- Are there any words that you don't know?
- Which words or groups of words seem powerful and why?

- What might be reasons why anyone would want to be a word hunter?
- What is the attraction of hunting for words? What would you do with them?
- What would you add to the collection if you were to start one of your own?
- How might you use the word hunter's collection in your own writing?

CREATING METACOGNITIVE AWARENESS OF WORD CHOICE

Creating excitement and awareness is the key concept at the beginning of the year. Why would we want to pay attention to words? What kinds of words do authors use? The point is that we want word consciousness to permeate the classroom. When students come to class unaware of recycling, we might make a conscious effort to teach and reinforce this concept. We discuss why it is important, point out when it is appropriate to do it and how others do it, and explicitly encourage this action. We want a similar effort to go into teaching and reinforcing word consciousness. Part of a recycling effort is making it easy for students to do it. This has to be considered in a word-consciousness effort as well. When students are reading at an independent level, the book or material should be at a level that is just right for them. If the material they read is too hard, too many words will be unfamiliar, and the search for Gifts of Words will be a frustrating experience. If the material has constrained vocabulary, chances are that the author isn't using very many Gifts of Words. However, many picture books and magazines, how-to books, and informational books from science and social studies can be appropriate reading material for gathering Gifts of Words.

An important insight for students is that not all published authors use language equally well. When Teresa was reading a book aloud one day, the students began to notice that the writing was relatively flat and boring. They requested another read-aloud because this author "didn't do a very good job of painting vivid images." Getting students to the point where they critically analyze an author's style is exciting!

Withdrawing From the Word Bank

We explicitly encourage students to "borrow" the gifts that authors give readers—phrases that are enticing or that create a vivid illustration for the reader—so that they can learn to use this style of discourse to express mood, create interest, and build their own stories. Through this appropriation of phrases, the novice writers become aware of how these types of gifts might sound in their own writing. In other words, the vocabulary, phrases, and sentences that add depth to a story are explicitly pointed out as language that could be adapted or personalized in students' own attempts to communicate through written narratives or reports. As you can see in Figure 2-2, words and phrases enter the Bank of Powerful Language through reading activities and are then available for use in individual, small-group, and whole-class writing projects.

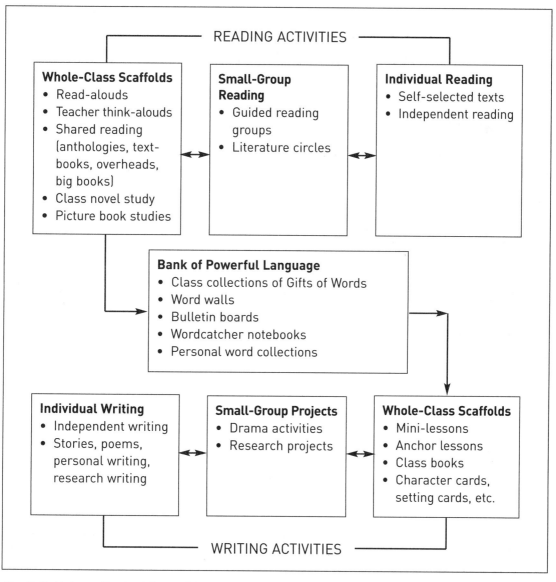

Fig. 2-2: Using a Bank of Powerful Language

We are careful to discuss how this appropriation is a step toward developing their own phrases and Gifts of Words for readers.

Some teachers worry that using phrases from published books in one's own writing is a form of plagiarizing. At this point, yes—they are using the words of other authors. And we discuss with the students that it is important to acknowledge the original authors. However, artists learn particular techniques by copying the work of masters. This is also the case with writing. Students need a chance to copy the masters. If an artist produces a forgery with the intent to defraud, it is illegal. Similarly, plagiarism carries the intent to pass off the work as one's own. However, the purpose of the exercise of using Gifts of Words and children's authors as models for good writing is to teach the techniques of good writing. Imitation is reemerging as a valued aspect of composition (Butler, 2002). When writers imitate other authors, they become familiar with the style and form of that writing. Using the phrases from another author allows novice writers to capture nuances of language that they may not be able to generate for themselves. This is a phase of approximation that is valuable for developing expertise as a writer.

Over the year you'll see an exciting aspect of language use develop from this practice: students begin to personalize the "borrowed" phrases and use them more for prompting their own creations than borrowing them verbatim. "She was a great potato of a woman," from *Tuck Everlasting* by Natalie Babbitt, became "He was a long string bean of a man." "Pink is the daughter of red," from *Hailstones and Halibut Bones* by Mary O'Neill, became "Laughter is the big sister of a giggle."

Remember, paying attention to effective language is an emphasis of this whole program; therefore, talking about why a certain phrase is worth collecting and using is essential. This helps students identify strong verbs, adverbs, and nouns. We do not want our students to believe that flowery, overly descriptive language is the only effective way to write, but we do want them to think about the effect their word choice has on their reader's understanding and enjoyment.

Out of these word choice discussions, many mini-lessons arise, such as: What is an adverb? Where and when are adverbs used? Can you find any other examples of an adverb used effectively? Sometimes the discussions center on the feeling or memories certain Gifts of Words evoke. It is not necessary to overanalyze the language. In fact, it should be avoided. The focus is on the magic of language and the creation of a safe environment in which students are encouraged to experiment with words. Experimentation with language in an atmosphere where they can learn without fear of ridicule is key. Throughout all of this instruction, the elements of the writing process are intact (see Calkins, 1986) and are explained more fully in Chapters 6 through 9.

Logistics of Using the Bank of Powerful Words

The purpose of this Bank of Powerful Language is to provide a resource for students to use in their own writing. When they are crafting a story and want to enhance the description of a character, they can take a set of character descriptions to their desk and gather ideas and phrases they might like to use. They might develop a character like Herman E. Calloway in *Bud, Not Buddy*, a "grouchy old bald-headed guy with a tremendous belly" (Curtis, 1999, p. 172) or Agnes in *The Great Gilly Hopkins*, "a shriveled-up-looking little sixth grader . . . with long red hair that fell greasily to her waist" (Paterson, 1987, p. 26).

However, we need to create both the context for using the bank and a system for finding appropriate Gifts of Words. Gifts of Words can be gathered from any genre that the students want to write. Once gathered, they are ready for use. A simple way to start is to develop a mock-up paragraph using the gathered words and phrases.

CREATING A MOCK-UP PARAGRAPH

In this activity, students work in groups with large chart paper. They put "Powerful Language" in the center of a web and then record words and phrases that they would like to use in their own writing. This same process, focused more narrowly on descriptions of the main characters, or of settings, can be used to circumscribe the range of the selections.

After developing each web, students write a short paragraph or a few sentences using some of the powerful language the class has collected. This gives them a scaled-down opportunity to approximate literary discourse styles. At this point, however, do not expect amazing sentences from everyone. This process of focusing on language use intensely is often a new way of thinking about writing for students.

ILLUSTRATING THE GIFTS OF WORDS

To become more familiar with the Gifts of Words used by a particular author, each student chooses his or her favorite Gift of Words from the novel and illustrates it. This activity makes concrete the images that the words create. At this point, it is important to recognize differences in students' experiences and understanding of the concept of powerful language. Some students seem to start by identifying literal images; it takes time and experience before they are able to recognize figurative language.

For example, in Bonnie's class, one student chose to illustrate the powerful phrase "the waters were still and speckled gold with the sun." Another student chose to illustrate the phrase "he tripped." Both created an image, but the latter is more literal. "He tripped" does not, on the surface, appear to be an example of powerful language. However, students are at different stages in their awareness of the concept of powerful language use. For this English language learner, "he tripped" created a recognizable, vivid image. Throughout the year, students' sophistication in identifying Gifts of Words will grow as they develop word consciousness.

AN ORGANIZATIONAL SYSTEM

Our students gather Gifts of Words using a writer's notebook, a wordcatcher notebook, and sticky notes. As they read or listen to stories, students collect Gifts of Words until they have gathered 10 to 12 excerpts. At this point, they select their two favorites and record them on long strips of construction paper or tagboard. These are then added to the Bank of Powerful Language so that all students can see and use them. Attaching sticky magnets to the back of each strip works well because the strips are easily displayed on a magnetic blackboard and can be taken down for individual use.

The volume of Gifts of Words strips can become a management problem. The purpose for having them on strips is to keep the words and phrases "in their face" and visible. If they are put in files, the students do not use them. Put them out in plain view and students will easily borrow them, often without even leaving their desks. But there is a limit to the number that can be displayed. At first, we keep some on bulldog clips. Later, we gather the strips that are well used, and group them into the following categories: feelings, actions, similes, setting, and character. Each category is coil-bound to make a booklet that is hung in plain view.

Oh, Those Gifts of Words! Keeping the Idea Fresh

There needs to be a constant supply of fresh Gifts of Words. Therefore, the collecting and selection of items for the word bank continues throughout the year. For instance, while students are reading a class novel or reading an independent novel, ask them to list Gifts of

Words on chart paper and then give each student three stickers to place beside their favorites. The Gifts of Words that receive the most votes are then recorded and added to the bank. Another quick way to select the most popular is to have a thumbs-up/thumbs-down vote and keep only the ones with a high vote count.

At times throughout the year, students' familiarity with the Gifts of Words falters. We want to reacquaint them with what is displayed in the bank, so we created a Gifts of Words Bingo game. The strips are displayed in rows so all the students can see them. Each student secretly chooses three for the game and writes them down as his or her "board" (see Figure 2-3). As a caller points to each of the Gifts of Words strips randomly, the students check it off. The first student to check all three on his or her list calls "Bingo." The caller gives the student one of the Gifts of Words that they must put in a sentence. If it is done to everyone's satisfaction, the student becomes the next caller. Students begin a new game by choosing different Gifts of Words.

Gifts of Words	Game #1	Game #2	Game #3
"her tears worming down her face" *Esperanza Rising*, p. 92			
"the mean, skinny, narrow-eyed boys" *Bridge to Terabithia*, p. 36			
"waddling out to us, oozing maternal noises" *The Trolls*, p. 43			

Fig. 2-3: Student's Bingo Board

Thoughts to Ponder

We are often asked at workshops whether our students collect Gifts of Words every day and how many they collect. The key here is not how many they collect but what is done with the collection. At the beginning of the year we collect them at every opportunity. Then, throughout the year, we become more selective and collect only when needed or when a student comes across a particularly effective Gift of Words. At one point in the year, we noticed that students were going to the bank and taking nothing back to their desks. When asked about this, they said that there was nothing useful. It was clear to us that we needed to generate more "useful" strips.

By actively encouraging the appropriation of literary styles and words, we can also see when students don't quite understand the nuances of particular words. Students wrote the following sentences:

> "I couldn't see the mouse very well. Therefore I went to the basement to get a preferable look at the mouse from underneath." (Jomal, grade 5)

> "In recent times, my sister walked up to me and alleged, 'It's time for bed.'" (Amandip, grade 6)

This creates a marvelous teachable moment where we can explore, with the student, their intent and discuss how the word they chose didn't fit the meaning intended. We do not find this disturbing and, in fact, celebrate the risks these students are taking. Short and Burke (1989) say that "the world learners live in is an ambiguous one in which there are few right or wrong answers. They must therefore become risk takers who are willing to live with ambiguity and its consequences. . . . Although it is natural for learners to feel tension in an ambiguous world, that tension is counterproductive if it leads to stress. Students feel stress when the consequences of being wrong are too great to risk a mistake" (p. 198). We enjoy observing the struggle and the conscientious effort these students are making to improve as writers.

Out of the Mouths of Learners

It is always informative to ask students what they think about their learning, and whether what they have done in the classroom is useful for them. When asked to talk about the Gifts of Words, the students in Bonnie's sixth-grade class had no difficulty knowing what they were. Sandra said, "They don't just say, 'Oh, she's got nice hair,' they say, 'She's got hair that's as white as snow,' or something, so it describes more about the hair." Ari gave an example: "It describes, like, say, crying: 'Tears were coming down his cheeks as his head was on his knees.'" And Roberto concurred, "It gives you a better picture in your head of it, like, say, crying, 'Tears were pouring from his eyes.' You get a better picture."

Tiffany's answers to interview questions also show how writing changed. When asked if this year had been the same for her as other years, she replied, "The work's different. This year we're doing all this language stuff. At first I didn't really like it but then, as I wrote more, I started to like it more."

These were her responses to other interview questions:

In which area do you think you are the most successful this year at school?
"I would have to say the Gifts of Words. At the beginning of the year, if I wanted to write a story, I didn't put much effort into it. And then after reading *Underground to Canada*, I came up with so many good Gifts of Words."

Did anything else help change your mind?
"Well, I just saw how other people's writing sounded so good and it just occurred to me to try it and then I tried it and I liked it."

So you think this helped you in your writing, then?
"Before, when I went to write a story, I didn't know what to put in a space. I'd put in something else and then it wouldn't sound as good. And then I'd put, like, a Gift of Words and it just makes the story stand out more."

The voice of this student points to the connection between the writing of a published author (Barbara Smucker, *Underground to Canada*), her classmates' writing, and this student's personal writing pieces. We also hear in her voice the understanding that writing needs to "sound" good both to the writer and to her audience.

If we had any doubts about the Gifts of Words as a focus for discussion and a bridge between the reading experiences and the writing experiences of the class, these interviews conducted after a year of the program convinced us that we were onto something exciting.

——— ❋ ———

Chapter 3

Playing With Words

Using Stand-Alone Games and Activities to Generate Enthusiasm

Who knows two one-syllable rhyming words that describe an overweight feline? (A fat cat.) What about a sneaky insect? (A sly fly.)

Succulent, savory, spicy words! Making learning fun is key to any teaching situation—and especially to language teaching. We feel a responsibility to instill what Bonnie labeled as a "curious wonderment" for learning. One way to generate enthusiasm and excitement about words is to create many opportunities to play with them in risk-free, safe, and nonevaluative settings. Word games can be inserted throughout the day: before lunch, in centers, after recess, or whenever you can squeeze them in. The following activities help develop conscious attention to words and their uses. Some of these activities are for the sheer fun of playing with words, while other activities are used to directly scaffold student writing. The key here is to find activities that you, as a teacher, think are fun. This list is not "the" magical one. There are many ways to play with language and any fun activity will do. Before long, you may find that you are inventing your own games and quizzes that play with words.

There are numerous books full of wonderful ideas and games for playing with language. There are also published games such as Scrabble, Boggle, and Balderdash where words are central to playing the game. However, the business of real reading and writing seemed so important and time was so precious in our classrooms that we shied away from the use of games, thinking that they might trivialize our program and fragment the students' attention.

In an era of accountability, where do games fit into the standards? Our experience with the games and the short introductory activities in this chapter has convinced us that games, when connected to real reading and writing, can provide important opportunities to help young writers as they learn to use their own voices in the writing classroom. Our classrooms were communities that had an identity created by the word-awareness focus. The students were conscious of it; we were immersed in thinking of ways to develop word awareness. As a consequence, things began to connect; ideas became related. Words, and looking at words, became a sort of glue that held our communities together.

Whole-Class Games

Many of these games take five to ten minutes and can be played at any time. In addition, they are great "sponge" activities to insert into the day. When you are waiting for an assembly to start or have a few minutes after cleanup, you can start Guess My Rule, begin an Add-On Story, or play Choke. These activities offer both amusement and cognitive challenges when there is a bit of transition time between subjects, or when a lesson goes more quickly than planned.

GUESS MY RULE

I'm going to Disneyland. Do you want to come, John? Yeah! Well, I'm Bonnie and I'm taking a banana. What are you going to take?

The object of this game is to figure out the rule and to provide an opportunity to think about words as individual units. In the example above, John names an item, and if the word begins with the same letter as his name (e.g., *Jell-O*), he gets to go. If he names an item that doesn't fit the rule, then of course he doesn't get to go to Disneyland. During each turn, students are required to remember all the previous items as well as provide a new item that they think will fit the rule. This is a great way to dismiss students, one at a time, to recess.

To start, the rule could be almost anything—for example, each item might have to follow alphabetical order, begin with the last letter of the item before, or have double consonants. As the students become more familiar with the game, the rules can start to reflect semantic categories such as types of animals or things found in the ocean, and the sentences can change to focus on other parts of speech such as verbs, adverbs, or adjectives (e.g., "I'm going to Disneyland. Do you want to come, John? Yeah! Well, I'm Bonnie and I'm biking there. How about you?").

ADD-ON STORY

An add-on story has a rich tradition. These are also called continuous stories or chain stories. Someone begins with a lead sentence such as, "Last night as I crept down the hall and out the back door…" or "A really weird thing happened to me on the way home from school. I…." The story is continued by each student adding something. Our twist is that the thing you add focuses on word consciousness and use of powerful language. For instance, students add a descriptive phrase that uses a powerful verb, or they have to use an adjective to describe a noun in their phrase. To scaffold word learning, you may want to brainstorm a chart of powerful verbs or adjectives students can refer to as they play this game. Reluctant participants are allowed to pass in the beginning. However, as this becomes a more common activity, reluctant participants often use phrases they've heard others use in a previous rendition. This becomes a safe way to contribute to the story and to develop ownership of words.

CHOKE

Most people have trouble thinking when they are put on the spot under a time crunch. When their minds stop working, they "choke." Students like this challenge in a fun, friendly, accepting environment. The task is simple: in 60 seconds, tell all the words you know that start with a given letter. No one can help the challenger and no proper names can be used. You can adapt the letter given to match the language proficiency of the student. Thus, an English language learner can be given a relatively easy letter, like *B*, and a student with a wide vocabulary can be given letters such as *Q* and *Z*. This game can be adapted in several directions. Students can name categories, such as verbs starting with the letter *R*, geology words, adjectives used to describe people, or any other category you want them to explore. Whatever category you choose, we think that your students will enjoy the excitement of the game. Other students can think of several words in the category, and they often think they can do better than the challenger until the clock starts ticking for them. A variation with less pressure on individual performance allows small groups to cogenerate the words. They can then try to beat their own record in 60 seconds.

SHADES OF MEANING

The Shades of Meaning activity emerged from a Synonym Wheel activity, where a commonly used word (e.g., *big*, *hot*, *mad*, *said*) was put into the center of a wheel, and the spokes became words that could be used instead of the more common word (e.g., *large*, *huge*, *enormous*, *giant*). However, in discussion with another group of teachers, we realized that these were not actually synonyms but various shades of meaning. Erik Blomquist, a fourth-grade teacher, took this idea and created a tree in his room with brown construction paper as the trunk. You can copy leaves, such as the one in Figure 3-1 (which you can use as a master), cut them out, and attach them to the tree. In the middle of each leaf, put a commonly used word that has many other, more descriptive words that show the various shades of meaning for that concept: words such as *cold*, *hot*, *big*, *little*, *talk quietly*, *talk loudly*, *walk quickly*, and *walk slowly* work well for this activity. Discuss the idea that other words can be related to these words along continuums of meaning

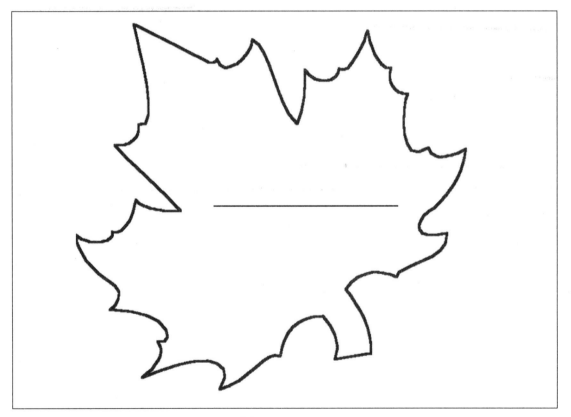

Fig. 3-1: Leaf for Shades of Meaning Activity

(e.g., *frigid* means very cold, *cool* means slightly cold). Have students brainstorm different shades of meaning for each leaf, and write new words and phrases on the leaf with the common word as they find them. This provides another type of word bank to use in their writing.

Playing with the Shades of Meaning can take many forms. One game asks students to identify the appropriate category for a given word. To start, choose some relatively unknown words related to words on the tree (e.g., *blistering* for *hot*). If a student or table group says *hot* and uses it appropriately in a sentence, they get a point. After they use it, ask if they knew the answer or guessed. If they guessed, ask them to verbalize the clues they used to get the answer. For instance, they could have guessed *hot* by connecting the idea of getting a blister when you touch something hot to *blistering*. In another activity, words from a leaf (or two leaves with words at opposite ends of a spectrum, such as *hot* and *cold*) are distributed to students on 3" x 5" cards. They then form the continuum by standing in a line with their words, which represent points along the continuum (e.g., *frigid, cool, warm, boiling*). Discussions of whether *huge* is bigger or smaller than *giant* or *colossal* are rich expressions of word consciousness.

Reinforcing Particular Concepts or Words With Games

There are often terms in a unit that we want students to learn, terms that we need to talk about language use, or terms that we are learning as shades of meaning for more common terms. The next two games require a bit of preparation, but the result is well worth it. Students enjoy this type of practice much more than filling in worksheets.

WORD JEOPARDY

You can create a Word Jeopardy game with any type of content. For instance, you may want to build on the Shades of Meaning activity above by using the commonly used words on the tree as the category headings. To play, the students work in table groups and can consult each other to develop the answer. A table team gets to pick, for instance, Cold Words for 100, and when you read that item, the word is *icy*. They need to define it and use it well in a sentence. A Cold Word for 1,000 points might be a word like *glacial*.

To develop the cards, choose the category headings from your Shades of Meaning tree. Then look in the thesaurus and rank the six words from most common to least common. The most common (e.g., *icy*) have lower points than the least common words (e.g., *glacial*). A thesaurus is a useful tool for developing this game. You can arrange the categories as you wish, in a grid across the blackboard. List the amount for each word inside the grid. When students pick a category and amount, erase that square and write in the word.

Cold	Hot	Said	Walk
icy	100	100	100
200	200	*whispered*	200
300	300	300	300
500	500	500	*sprint*
750	*scalding*	750	750
glacial	1,000	1,000	1,000

RICOCHET

Much like the idea of Word Jeopardy, the purpose of this game is to reinforce some content or terms that we want our students to know. Each student is given at least one card. The purpose is to whip around the room quickly with responses and new questions. There is an answer at the top of each card and a question at the bottom. If a student has an answer for the question asked, she or he responds, "I have…" and then asks a question: "Who has . . . ?"

MATERIALS

You will need the same number of 3" x 5" cards as the number of students playing the game. Each student needs to have a unique card. For example, if there are 30 students in the class, use thirty 3" x 5" cards. On the top of each card, write "I have… " in black marker, and about halfway down the card write "Who has…?" Once this is done, set the cards aside.

I have…	I have…	I have…
Who has…?	Who has…?	Who has…?

The finished product will look like the cards that follow.

I have... Words that sound the same but have different meanings **Who has...?** Simile	**I have...** Comparisons using the words *like* or *as* **Who has...?** Alliteration	**I have...** Repeating the first letter or word in connected words **Who has...?** Homonyms

For this game to work, the questions and answers must be in a continuous loop. The easiest way to organize the cards is to create a master set of the questions and answers. Number a sheet of paper in rows, creating as many rows as cards. In two columns at the top, write "I have . . ." and "Who has . . . ?" The example below creates only three cards, but the process is the same for any number of cards.

Card #	I have . . .	Who has . . . ?
Card 1	Words that sound the same but have different meanings	Simile
Card 2	Comparisons using the words *like* or *as*	Alliteration
Card 3	Repeating the first letter or word in connected words	Homonyms

Start with the first and last rows. Write the question (Who has . . . ?) in the second column on the bottom row (Homonyms). Write the answer (Words that sound the same but have different meanings) at the top of the first card (I have . . .). Then continue writing the rest of your questions and answers on the sheet. When the sheet is complete, transfer the content onto the cards you've already made.

HOW TO PLAY

Once all cards are filled in, they are ready for use. After the cards are shuffled, each student gets one card. Pick a student to start by reading only the question on the bottom half of his card (Who has . . . ?). Whoever has the answer calls out, "I have . . ." and quickly reads the bottom half of her card (Who has . . . ?). The game ends when all questions have been asked or you run out of time. The purpose is to go through the cards as quickly as possible, as the game's name, Ricochet, implies. Talking about the meaning of *ricochet* and how the name fits the game will also raise word consciousness about titles, and may add another word to students' vocabulary. Timing the class adds an incentive and lots of fun.

At the end, collect the cards. Storing the cards in a resealable plastic bag helps keep the set intact, which is important for the game to work as intended. Students can develop their own sets, and you can use this game to reinforce word meanings in any subject area, such as social studies, science, or math. Any time students are required to learn a set of facts, Ricochet makes learning fun.

WORD IDOL

The purpose of this game is to point out that people actually use many different types of words (even ones the students might think are too academic to be used often), to provide another context for their use, and to become aware of the multiple ways a word can be used. Bill Nagy developed the idea for this game, based on the television show *American Idol*.

MATERIALS

Students need access to the Internet to play this game. The teacher chooses six relatively unusual words from a unit being studied (e.g., *exoskeleton, crustacean, aquatic, mollusk, invertebrate, unsegmented*). Be sure the words aren't product names.

HOW TO PLAY

Groups of students hypothesize how frequently each word is used on the Internet and decide which ones they think will be the two most and the two least frequently used words. Frequency is determined by the number of hits on Google (e.g., *exoskeleton* has 1,050,000 hits; *unsegmented* has 263,000). After the groups rank the words, a team of judges searches Google for each word, reports the frequency, and reads one phrase using each of the words. The teacher records the actual ranking, and points are awarded if a team's ranking matches the actual ranking by Google. One point is given for each correct match. The first team that reaches 20 points becomes the team to search the Internet for the next game. As a variation, teams of students can choose the words to look up.

Games for Small Groups

Some games, including many board games, work better in smaller groups. These games can be used in centers, during free choice, or during Friday afternoon sessions. We're sure you can think of many more, but here are our favorites.

TRIADS

Triads is a wonderful way to teach students about the multiple meanings of words and to encourage critical thinking skills. It is a word category game—lots of fun for any age group! We learned this game by sitting around Judy's dining room table with Bill Nagy. Bill taught this game, which he learned from Steve Scanley in high school, to his colleagues at the Center for the Study of Reading at the University of Illinois.

MATERIALS

This game requires from four to eight people, so you can use it as a center or have several games going at once in the room. Each player thinks of a category with no fewer than four and no more than nine items in it (e.g., the planets, joints in the body, the names of the dwarfs in *Snow White*, or North American bears). Three words from the category are chosen and written secretly on three separate slips of paper. Small pieces of card stock work best, if available. Each person needs three pieces of paper each time the game is played. A variety of writing utensils helps disguise students' writing so that cards are matched by category, not pen color.

HOW TO PLAY

The object of the game is to collect sets of three cards of the same category. This means that students have to figure out the categories represented by the cards in their hands, and to lay down correct sets of three cards to get points.

One person collects all the cards, shuffles them, and deals three cards to each player. Each player looks at his cards and tries to figure out what the categories might be (players keep their guesses to themselves). For example:

POLAR	ANKLE	GOLDEN

[bears? others: grizzly? panda?]   [joints? bracelets?]   [no idea!]

The player to the right of the dealer starts by saying, for example, "Myra, do you have *panda*?" If Myra has a *panda* card, she gives it to the "asking" player and that player has a second turn. The "asking" player continues to ask as long as she is asking the right person for the right card. If Myra does not have *panda*, the turn moves to the next player. The cards people ask for provide clues about what might be in their hands. For example, if player number 3 asks for *grizzly*, then she may have another type of bear card.

When everyone has had a turn, each player passes one of his cards to the right and the game continues. The passing of a card happens after each round. One point is awarded each time a person collects all three cards in the original category. If the category is correct, both the player and the originator or author of the set receive a point. However, one point is deleted if a player's category is discovered first or last, and no player can declare her own original set. This helps students choose "in-the-middle" categories that are neither too hard nor too easy. There may be times when a player has no cards and others have more than three cards. This is fine, as both types of players can continue asking for cards and are full members of the game.

SILLY STORIES

Students often enjoy creating silly stories, much like creating Mad Libs. In Mad Libs, students list interesting nouns, verbs, adjectives, and adverbs without a story context. The Mad Lib stories are then filled in using the generated words.

The Silly Stories activity is a variation on the theme of pulling together disparate ideas to create a story. The object is to construct a plausible narrative using randomly drawn cards as a story starter.

MATERIALS

Eight to ten words or phrases for each of the four categories of character, setting, plot, and mood are either brainstormed or chosen from the Bank of Powerful Language. These are written on card stock and stored in separate envelopes labeled by category on the outside.

HOW TO PLAY

Students, working in groups, randomly choose a card from each of the envelopes. In choosing, they come up with some amusing combinations, such as a *scruffy old pirate*, *in a cafeteria*, *theft*, *as soft as a pillow*. They then need to construct a story using those concepts and words.

When several groups are working on these stories at the same time, we set a time limit and have them move to another group's story after ten minutes. They read what the first group has written and figure out how to continue the second story while another group adds to their original start. After a few rotations where they add to various stories, the final group adds a concluding sentence, and the stories are read aloud. Students are amused to see how their original ideas developed. The stories are often very funny, sometimes silly, but definitely entertaining.

Games to Play Alone or in Pairs

There are many activities students can do alone or in pairs. They can do (or develop) cross-word puzzles and word searches, think of word rebus puzzles, or experiment with language and manipulate words for fun.

PALINDROMES

A palindrome is a word or phrase that can be read the same in either direction. The term *race car* is a palindrome. So is the phrase *never odd or even*. One fun activity is to have students try to find or create palindromes. In addition, there are palindrome squares that can be read in either direction in any row or column. Student can try to create these, too, although it is hard to do!

N	E	T
E	Y	E
T	E	N

CREATING WORD REBUSES

Word rebuses (Espy, 1975) are visual interpretations of common phrases, such as a hole in one:

or a square meal: M E
                      A L

Terry Stickels (2006) calls them Frame Games and has published them widely. Students love solving these puzzles and creating them for each other.

AMASS A MASS OF WORDS

One interesting way to focus on words is to have students collect various types of words. For instance, they can be given a handout with categories like these:

Noisy Words	Quiet Words	Words That Sound Like an Action	Night Sounds	Daytime Sounds
shrill whistle	gurgling brook	buzz	muffled beat of bat wings	traffic whizzing by

As students find these words by brainstorming with family members, looking in books, or asking friends, the words go up on a chart. Then you can discuss the words and phrases and add them to your Bank of Powerful Language.

Thoughts to Ponder

Children learn through play, and these games work on multiple levels. They provide the context for developing metacognitive awareness about words as well as provide a challenging and interesting way to introduce and reinforce vocabulary. While they are engaging in these activities, students are building a supportive and interactive community that encourages word exploration and use.

An advantage to using games such as the ones in this chapter is that you can adapt them to the students in your class. No two classes are identical, and each year you have a range of experience and knowledge. Challenging students within their ZPD, in a safe and fun environment, with scaffolding to build success by working in groups and allowing much discussion, can help create excitement and establish students' identities as people who like words.

Of course, you need to use these games judiciously. Sprinkling them into your curriculum works better than trying to use them all at once. However, we recommend at least one word-consciousness game per week to create a lighthearted, entertaining arena for alluring and appealing amusement.

—— ✳ ——

Chapter 4

Books, Books, Books

Building Word Consciousness Through Read-Alouds and Shared Reading

As you have probably noted from previous chapters, books are the center of our program—all kinds of wonderful, delicious books. We use books for everything. They are our touchstones, our models, and our inspirations. Picture books, poetry books, novels, and nonfiction books are gathered from libraries, bookstores, discount tables, and garage sales. One of the most enjoyable aspects of our research group was sharing our latest finds. We developed favorite authors, argued over intended meaning, and even wrote to an author to see which of us was right!

Our stance is very similar to the unit of study approach described by Nia (1999). Both approaches study elements of writing through examining the moves professional authors use. We both delve into an author's craft to improve student writing. Unlike Nia's approach, however, we are concentrating on the vocabulary and phrasing authors use, in particular, as well as the overall quality of the literature. Our read-aloud and shared texts are chosen with these guidelines in mind:

- You love the text.
- It is a juicy text with much to talk about in terms of content.
- It contains vivid language and interesting words.

Because books are central to this program, it is essential for us to expand on how you can use these cherished volumes to develop word consciousness in your classrooms.

Learning Vocabulary Through Read-Alouds

Read-aloud is the context in which we show very explicitly the power of language to move and inform the reader. We are excited, tearful, overjoyed, and despondent as the characters in our read-aloud novel experience the ups and downs of the story. Not many of us can get to the end of *Charlotte's Web* or *I Am David* without a lump in the throat. "Are you all right, Ms. Wells?" asked Alexander as Jan finished the latter novel, in which David is reunited with his mother after a long and exhausting journey across postwar Europe. As we listen to a historical event, read aloud by a teacher who has enthusiasm and delight in the subject, we are transported to that time and place and can visualize the experience. We travel to other countries, even to outer space and back, all in the time it takes to read about it. Facts are brought to life when they are shared through the medium of reading aloud. When you read to children, it is a priceless gift and a prime teaching tool.

In 1985, the National Academy of Education report proclaimed that "the single most important activity for building the knowledge required for eventual success in reading is reading to children" (Anderson, Hiebert, Scott, & Wilkinson, 1985). Since then, there have been several studies indicating that children as young as preschool age learn new words when books are read aloud to them (Elley, 1989; Penno, Wilkinson, & Moore, 2002; Robbins & Ehri, 1994). The language in children's books is more complex and contains more rare words than expert-witness testimony in court, college graduates talking to friends or spouses, or prime-time adult television shows (Hayes & Ahrens, 1988).

Read-aloud allows us to "think aloud": to wonder, question, infer, connect, and evaluate ideas so that we show our students what those strategies look like. In her book *Nonfiction Writing From the Inside Out*, Laura Robb (1994) calls the think-aloud "making the mysterious visible." She finds think-alouds valuable because "they construct for students a tangible mental model of ideas that are often elusive for them, such as organizing information into a compare/contrast structure" (p. 44).

We found that our focus on language led us to think aloud continually about words: the meaning of words, the placing of words together for effect, the sound of words, and the connections between words. We became adept at stopping briefly to muse about words, trying not to interrupt the flow of the reading too much, but involving the class in active thinking as they listened.

Reading aloud to students also allows us the privilege of modeling our belief that reading is a great way to spend time—a magical, life-changing experience. Our passion for reading can only really be communicated when we read aloud. We choose those texts to read to the class that will build a classroom culture. The texts we read together take on a special meaning in the life of that classroom. Our children are only once the perfect age to hear *Charlotte's Web* read aloud; only once are they poised perfectly to be enchanted by *James and the Giant Peach.* As we read *The Giver,* we know that this book makes our 10-year-old students think about the world they live in like no other book does. When we read with passion, we delight in the language and roll our tongues around the delicious words. Whether we are reading poetry, novels, picture books, or nonfiction material, the read-aloud time is priceless for vocabulary learning.

FINDING THE PERFECT READ-ALOUD BOOKS

Choose texts that offer powerful language to their readers. It is important to find those books that work for you. You, as reader, need to be able to roll the words off the tongue with delight, so some research in the library is important. *The Reading Teacher,* an International Reading Association journal, offers both children's and teachers' choices each year, and it is worthwhile seeking out those recommendations that are made by students and teachers. Similarly, some of the classic Newbery Award winners make exceptional read-alouds. We love Kate DiCamillo's *The Tale of Despereaux: Being the Story of a Princess, Some Soup, and a Spool of Thread* (who wouldn't be intrigued by the title?), which won the Newbery in 2004, and *Whittington,* the 2006 award-winner by Alan Armstrong. Teacher-librarians are great resources for suggestions of picture books, novels, short stories, and poetry books that have particularly powerful language. At the end of this book, we have included a bibliography of children's books that we have found particularly successful in our classrooms. This, like any bibliography, is a personal selection. As you begin to develop a word-conscious classroom you will probably add other books that you enjoy. All of us begin to look at old favorites with new eyes, with a focus on the rich vocabulary they contain.

You can add to the class word bank with every read-aloud session, being ever watchful for Gifts of Words. This is particularly important early in the year and may taper off to fewer additions during the year. Please refer back to the Chapter 2 section "Oh, Those Gifts of Words! Keeping the Idea Fresh" for ideas to use as the year progresses.

USING THINK-ALOUDS TO HIGHLIGHT VOCABULARY

Here is an example of thinking aloud to find Gifts of Words. The focus of the lesson is the author's use of metaphor and simile. The book is *Like Butter on Pancakes* by Jonathan London. As you read, stop periodically and reflect on the language, making your own thinking clear. Finally, ask the students to notice the language and tell what they thought was interesting about it.

MATERIALS

Prepare the book with sticky notes, marking appropriate stopping places.

WHAT TO DO

As you read, make your thoughts visible to your students. Here is an example of how Jan uses think-alouds:

> *I'm going to read aloud from a book with very special language. It's a lovely story about a boy waking up and hearing all sorts of sounds. Just listen to how the author helps us to hear the sounds the boy hears: "Beyond the rim of morning the sun ticks, the birds talk and the spoons sleep nestled in the kitchen drawers. First light melts like butter on pancakes, spreads warm and yellow across your pillow."*
>
> *When I hear the words "the sun ticks," I think of a clock ticking. I think about how the sun is like a clock, moving across the sky as the day passes. When the day is over, night falls, and it gets dark. So the author thinks of the sun like a clock telling us that time is passing during the day.*
>
> *[Jan reads another sentence.] "After supper the night creeps in and the moon spills milk for the cat to drink." When I read this, I think about a pool of spilled milk, all white and glistening. The author makes me think that the moonlight must be very bright and that it looks like a puddle of milk on the floor. It paints a really vivid picture in my mind. Listen to some more of the story and let's see if there are any more examples of this powerful language. I'll read really slowly, and you can put up your hand if you hear a Gift of Words.*

As she reads, the students listen and raise their hands. Jan writes the Gifts of Words on a chart and discusses the reasons for their choices. At the end of the lesson she adds the Gifts of Words to the Bank of Powerful Language.

LESSONS TO ENHANCE READING ALOUD

The following four lessons use reading aloud to connect very purposefully to the writing workshop. After each of these activities, the students are ready to write. They are enthusiastic, eager, and primed with good ideas. The first uses the visualization technique Sketch to Stretch. The second utilizes the semantic web, cocreated in response to the read-aloud. The third uses clues from the text presented prior to reading to predict and anticipate a story. The fourth, Sort and Predict, uses vocabulary selected from the story upon which predictions can be built.

Using Visualization: Connecting Art and Vocabulary Through Reading Aloud

The read-aloud time is an ideal opportunity to encourage and develop our students' abilities to visualize the events, characters, settings, and emotions in a story. There are various versions of the visualization strategy. Harste, Short, and Burke called it "Sketch to Stretch" in their seminal book, *Creating Classrooms for Authors* (1988, pp. 353–354).

In their version, students are divided into groups of four or five. They read a selection (from a common text), then draw a sketch of "what the selection meant to you or what you made of the reading." After the sketches are complete, each student shares his drawing and the others say what they think the artist is attempting to say. The artist gets the last word.

We use a variation of this technique during read-aloud. The students have a piece of plain paper folded into six boxes. At strategic points in a story, we stop and ask the students to draw what they see in their mind's eye. "Imagine you have a video playing in your brain. What pictures do you see?" As they draw, they recall what has been read and embellish their drawing with details from the story. After each stopping point, the students share their drawings with a partner. The whole class discusses what has happened, what might happen, and what they learned by drawing the picture, and the story then moves on. The power of this strategy is that it deepens comprehension and helps all the students come to a place of common understanding.

Our colleague Alan Jones took this one stage further and linked the sketching and visualization to the writing process. Teaching a grade 3/4 class, he observed their writing to be event driven (the "and then . . ." syndrome) and typically flat, lacking in emotion. The revision stage of the writing process was difficult for most of the children. They focused only on the technical errors (spelling, punctuation) and were reluctant to make substantive changes to their writing.

Alan wanted to encourage visualization, highlight the presence of rich language in books and the students' own writing, emphasize how authors convey emotion or mood through language, and use small chunks of writing for content revision. He began with literature that was rich in language and content. The children used art to represent their understanding of the literature. This pictorial representation became the medium for using rich language as the children wrote about their pictures.

MATERIALS

Select a well-written passage or chapter from the book you are reading aloud to the class. Make sure it can be easily visualized. Students will need paper and pencils for drawing as well as their writer's notebooks or folders.

WHAT TO DO

1. **Read and visualize.** Begin by reading the passage to the class. Ask the children to try to visualize the story as they hear it (play the movie in their heads). As they become practiced at this, ask them to identify those words and phrases that make it easy for them to visualize. List these in a prominent place.

2. **Draw.** Ask the children to draw the most powerful, lasting image from the selection that was read. This can be discussed. Why did they choose this image? What makes it powerful? Is it important to the plot? Does it have visual or emotional impact?

   The goal of the activity is to capture the children's personal understandings and emotional responses to the literature, rather than recalling specific detail or selecting the "right" answers.

   Give the class a fairly short time in which to draw—five or ten minutes at the most. This is a first draft and they will get an opportunity to add to it later.

3. **Write.** Ask the children to write a sentence or two that captures the essence of their image. Again, give a short period of time—it is only a first draft.

4. **Revise the Writing.** Have the students work with partners to revise their writing. The revision has two goals: to make additions (details, description) and to make changes (substituting more powerful language in the place of everyday language).

   At first they may need the support of teacher-guided revision. Give short, specific revision tasks for the partners to complete. For example: replace an action word in your sentence with a more powerful word; add a word to describe the action word; add a word or phrase that shows the mood or emotion; add some information that is in the picture but not yet in the writing.

Encourage the children to consult the picture as well as the author's words and phrases that were collected during reading, and to ~~borrow from each other~~.

Give lots of time for this stage—this is the place the students play with language.

5. **Revise the drawing.** Have the students work with partners to generate ideas for revising the drawing. In the writing stage, the writing reflected the essence of the drawing. Now that the writing has been enhanced through revision, the drawing may need some work to reflect the essence of the writing.

Encourage the students to look for ways to portray in their drawings the more abstract elements of the image such as mood, thoughts, or feelings.

6. **Publish and present.** Many times it may be preferable to stop at this stage and simply have the students share their draft art and writing and their revisions. This is a great opportunity for the class to hear the difference between the draft and the more powerful language of the revisions. It is also a time to gather ideas and vocabulary from each other.

On occasion, both the drawing and the writing can be taken to the published stage. One effective presentation idea is to use photographic mats to frame the artwork, with the writing mounted as a caption. The mats are fairly inexpensive and can be reused in the classroom.

7. **Evaluate.** After practicing the technique several times, it is appropriate to ask the students to go through the process to produce a revised sentence and drawing that will be evaluated. Generate a set of criteria for a successful piece of work. For example, they can determine whether a piece:

- Has revisions that improve the overall power of the sentence
- Uses powerful language
- Matches the art to the writing in tone and mood
- Describes the rationale for choosing a particular phrase to add to the writing

Post the criteria on the wall. Using these criteria, students can self-evaluate and finally receive a grade for their efforts based on your judgment.

Using the preceding technique, students created the following responses to Jack London's *The Call of the Wild*. As you can see, the improvement in the children's use of words is striking, and their writing was enhanced greatly by this attention to the powerful language used by the author in the novel. Notice how these children used more precise and vibrant words in their revisions. *Slashed* is more powerful than *cut*; *beat violently* more expressive than *hit*.

Draft: Curly passed the visios Husky it leaped and bit Curly and jumped back hit the ground and the rest of the Huskys moved in on the sled dog.
Revision: Curly passed by the vicious and mad Husky. He leaped and bit Curly from her eye to her jaw. She hit the ground with a painful moan as the rest of the sled dogs moved in on the wounded dog. (Jenna, grade 4)

Draft: Curly was killed in a fight and eaten by a pack of Huskeys.
Revision: Curly was torn from eye to jaw by a ferocious pack of Huskies. (William, grade 4)

Draft: Morgan hit Buck with a club.
Revision: Morgan beat Buck violently with a wooden club that made Buck bleed on his nose and head. (Brenda, grade 3)

Draft: A Husky cut a Newfoundland dog in a fight.
Revision: A husky slashed Curly. Curly fell to the ground and perished. (Hasse, grade 3)

Clustering Words From Text: Using a Semantic Web

This strategy also takes the experience of reading aloud to the class and moves it into a writing lesson. Again, the teacher chooses a powerful piece of writing. After reading aloud, words from the reading are recalled and recorded on the board. Other connected words are then clustered around those words to create a complex web. Using this web of words, the students write their own version of the story, poem, or information.

This strategy is a version of a "semantic web" such as the ones described by Stahl and Nagy (2006). In the example lesson, the focus was developing a sense of the setting and the atmosphere in a passage from a piece of literature. After the lesson, the class wrote their own version of the story they had heard, but from the perspective of one of the characters. Using Anne Holm's *I Am David*, the class clustered words and then wrote in the first person. This lesson took place in Jan's grade 5 classroom.

MATERIALS

This activity involves the selection of an evocative piece of literature or nonfiction text; in this case, the first section of Chapter 1 of *I Am David*. Students will need writing materials and the teacher uses a blackboard or whiteboard, chart paper, or an overhead to create the web in front of the class.

WHAT TO DO

The teacher reads the selection aloud without interruption, asking students to listen for and remember any interesting words. After the reading, she collects and organizes the words on a chart. When a student offers the first word, *soap*, the teacher puts it in the top right-hand corner of the chart. Listen to the dialogue as she continues:

TEACHER: Give me another word.

STUDENT: *Fat.*

TEACHER: Would you like me to put this near the first word? Does it connect in some way?

STUDENT: No, put it by itself.

TEACHER: Another word, please.

STUDENT: *Bottle.*

TEACHER: Where shall I put it?

STUDENT: Next to *soap.*

TEACHER: And you want it next to *soap* because . . . ?

STUDENT: Because the man gave David soap and a bottle of water.

STUDENT: Put *man* next to *fat.*

TEACHER: Because . . . ?

STUDENT: Because the man was fat with piggy eyes.

TEACHER: Shall I put *piggy eyes* too?

The class continued to collect words in this way. If there was no connection given, the new word was placed in its own space. If they could be connected, they were joined with a line. A web of interconnected words was built on the blackboard (see Figure 4-1).

When the class had contributed a sufficient number of words from the text, the teacher asked the class to connect the words in new ways. Using a different color chalk she connected words based on the meanings students found.

"*Moon* connects with *run* because he had to run quickly because the moon was shining."

"*Moon* connects with *food* because he saw the soup because of the moonlight."

"*Soap* connects with *hand* because he would not let go of the soap."

"*Wanted* connects with *soap* because he wanted soap."

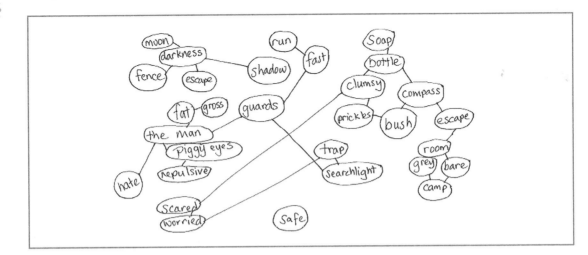

Fig. 4-1: Words Collected From Chapter 1, *I Am David,* by Anne Holm

When the web was finished, the students were given instructions for the writing task. This can be done on the same day or at a different time. If it is to be done later, the web must be kept on the board, or copied by the students onto paper.

CRITERIA FOR THE WRITING

Developing criteria for evaluation with students helps them understand the goals of their learning activities and move toward independence in evaluating their own work. The following criteria were developed for the writing that emerged from this activity:

- The setting comes to life through the use of powerful words.
- We can see the setting in our mind's eye.
- The language is vivid and descriptive; it uses ideas from the web.

These criteria then became the basis for evaluating the writing.

STUDENT REFLECTIONS

Another way to help students develop a metacognitive sense of word choice is to ask them to reflect on activities after their completion. In this case, when the writing was finished, we asked the students:

- Did making the web help you with your writing?

- Did you learn any new words or phrases that you will remember?
- Which words are you interested in collecting?

STUDENT EXAMPLES

I Am David—David's Perspective

When I woke up this morning I looked around my dark, grey, bare room that I knew so well. For twelve long years I've been in this jail. Actually, it is a jail camp with a barbed fence and guards that guard us like vultures. (Ayila, grade 5)

I Am David—Guard's Perspective

"Shh," I hissed to the boy sitting on the bed with his teeth clenched. His mouth dropped open as if a giant gorilla just tried to eat him. "Listen, I am going to help you escape from this smelly cramped place. When I light a match, you got a minute and a half, boy. Run like a madman to the prickle bush." (Liam, grade 5)

BUILDING FROM CLUES

This strategy is great fun and involves the students in predicting or guessing what might happen in a story. The teacher chooses objects that give clues as to the setting, characters, and events in a story that will be read. One by one, the objects are pulled from a bag or box, and the students try to guess their significance. This prereading discussion sets the stage for the reading that is to come.

MATERIALS

You will need several objects that give clues about a story; to highlight vocabulary, include several words from the story that may be unfamiliar to the class and write them on cards. You need four or five clues. Before reading *Solomon's Tree* by Andrea Spalding, Jan gathered some maple leaves and seeds (propellers), a photograph of a butterfly, and a First Nations carving. She selected the words *rustled*, *creaked*, *crashed*, and *sobbed*.

WHAT TO DO

Gather the students and show them the first clue. Be as dramatic as you wish to spark their imaginations. Individually, have them think about the object and what the story might be about. Then, have them discuss their ideas with a partner and ask them to share their ideas in the group. (This is called a think-pair-share strategy.) Show the second clue and use the same procedure to get them to think about how this new object might fit into the story. Continue to show the clues, one at a time, with students fitting each clue into their concept of the developing story. Be sure to give the students time to talk about their ideas before they draw and write to represent the story that they have built from the clues.

For example, when they saw the leaves and the seeds that Jan had gathered, the children said: "The story might have a tree in it. It could be fall and the tree is losing its leaves." When they read *rustled*, they said: "Maybe this is the sound of the leaves." The picture of the butterfly brought forth several suggestions:

"It's about a butterfly."

"The butterfly is in the tree."

"It could be about the life cycle."

Crashed and *sobbed* brought new thinking to the predictions:

"Maybe the tree fell on someone and made them cry."

And the mask made the class think about the possible setting:

"Is it in the museum?"

"Perhaps the people are First Nations?"

"Someone makes a mask from a tree."

CRITERIA FOR SUCCESS

The criteria for the written stories focus on comprehension, coherence in the writing, and word use. One goal is to help students use the clues to build a coherent and reasonable story with a problem and a resolution. Another goal is to help students incorporate words from the clues into the story. Thus, the evaluation of this writing is based on the degree to which students are able to create a story that is consistent with the clues and the key words that they were given, whether their stories are reasonable and coherent, and how they used words and images from the clues to enhance the story. Remember that these will not be perfectly polished pieces; these are opportunities for students to express their ideas in writing.

After the writing time, bring the class together to hear the published story you chose to read aloud. As you read, the class listens for the clues. Students enjoy comparing their stories with the one written by the published author.

Reflection provides an additional opportunity to scaffold students' thinking and to focus on word choices. These are some of the questions Jan asked students:

- What differences were there between your stories and the one we heard?
- What did the clues make you think about?
- Did the clues help you to make up a good story?
- Which Gifts of Words will you keep in your wordcatcher?
- Which Gifts of Words shall we put in the Bank of Powerful Language?

Sort and Predict Before Reading and Writing

Using *The King's Fountain* by Lloyd Alexander, illustrated by Ezra Jack Keats, this lesson took place in Jan's grade 5 classroom.

The warm-up activity chosen for this lesson was Sort and Predict (Brownlie & Close, 1992). Because there are a number of words that Jan felt might cause loss of comprehension, she created a sheet with key words on it that describe the characters. In this strategy, students create categories from the words they are given, and then use the words to predict what might happen in the story.

king	poor man
die of thirst	fountain
golden tongue	brave heart
learned scholar	wisdom
metalsmith	fearless
merchant	glib words
wrath	despair
hopeless	desperately
blurted	message
power	eloquence

Students read the words and discussed what they might mean. They cut up the words and sorted them into groups of four or five words. They were allowed to look at the book and see the pictures, but not to read the story. Dictionaries were used to clarify meanings. Here is one group's sorting:

People	Good Things	Bad Things	To Do With Talking	Odd One Out
poor man king metalsmith merchant learned scholar	brave heart wisdom fearless power golden tongue	despair desperately wrath hopeless die of thirst	blurted eloquence message glib words	fountain

Another group sorted this way:

Poor Man	King	Metalsmith	Merchant	Die of Thirst	Message
hopeless despair	power	brave heart fearless wrath wisdom	learned scholar eloquence golden tongue	desperately fountain	blurted glib words

After sorting all the words into categories, the groups made predictions about the story. They inferred from the words that they had worked with and from the pictures that this was some sort of legend or fable. Probably the poor man would turn out to be the hero of the tale, and it would have something to do with the king's power.

When Jan read the story aloud, showing the pictures, they discussed the story and the language used by the author. Some of the Gifts of Words they chose included:

For the splendor of his kingdom and the glory of his name (paints a picture)

He pondered lofty matters (strong way to describe the scholar)

Merchants whose words were as smooth as pearls and who could string them together endlessly (metaphor)

Smash every window, crack every wall (strong image)

Trudged home (strong verb)

I need only snap my fingers and my swordsmen will cut you to pieces (strong image)

They voted on which ones to add to the word bank.

In discussing the story, the class agreed that this story was full of Gifts of Words. They also noticed that there were a lot of words we don't use every day, but that the language in this story made it seem "long ago and far away."

This lesson was the perfect preparation for a writing activity involving character cards (described in Chapter 10). The language that described the poor man, the merchants, the scholar, and the metalsmith all helped to paint vivid images of the personalities, the strengths, and the weaknesses of these characters.

READ-ALOUD NONFICTION

Reading aloud from nonfiction can complement your social studies and science programs by exposing students to the concept words of the subject. In addition, read-alouds can help students discover the text features of informational writing that can aid their reading comprehension and nonfiction writing. When you read aloud you can show the students the following devices:

- Words in bold or italics that draw attention to ideas
- Pronunciation guides and phonetic spellings that show how a word sounds
- Information in text boxes or sidebars that adds to the main idea
- The table of contents that guides the reader to the chapter topics
- The index that guides the reader to specific information
- Glossaries that define and explain words found in the text
- Examples of the use of the writer's personal voice in sharing enthusiasm for the subject

However, some informational texts read as if the author is presenting a basket of facts instead of a well-written, coherent explanation. We have found it necessary to search for those informational books that are both well written and accurate. Picture books such as *The Wolf Girls: An Unsolved Mystery From History*, by Jane Yolen and Heidi Stemple, or *The Desert Is Theirs*, by Byrd Baylor, introduce rich language in the context of interesting information. There are several excellent resources for finding such books, including Daniel Kriesberg and Dorothy Frederick's *A Sense of Place: Teaching Children About the Environment With Picture Books*; the annual lists of Outstanding Science Trade Books for Students K–12, published by the National Science Teachers Association; and Notable Trade Books for Young People, published by the National Council for the Social Studies.

Instructions in textbooks, especially in mathematics, warrant particular attention. We often assume that students understand the vocabulary of instruction when, in fact, they do not. Academic words such as *compare*, *contrast*, and the like need special attention. This is particularly important for English language learners.

Here are some of the key questions for Unit I in the social studies textbook *Their Stories, Our History: Canada's Early Years* (Aitken et al., 2006).

- How did the First Nations belief systems differ from those of the first Europeans they encountered?
- How did First Nations and Europeans influence each other's cultures?
- How did Royal Government affect New France's development?

The verbs *differ*, *influence*, and *affect* are examples of academic key words that must be understood if the students are to think about the content of the questions. Read aloud key questions like these and think aloud the meaning of such important guiding words. For example, the teacher might say, "In question 1 I am thinking, what does *differ* mean? It means I have to look at two ideas and compare them. I must find things that are the same and things that are different. So I could use a T-chart while I'm reading to collect notes on these two ideas—the beliefs of First Nations and the beliefs of the Europeans."

Learning Vocabulary Through Shared Reading

Shared reading is a wonderful, warm, deliciously creative, and delightful whole-class activity. During shared reading, teacher and students read the same text together. Sometimes this is a big book, sometimes it is text on an overhead, or it can be material in an anthology or textbook. The teacher and class read together, taking turns or speaking simultaneously. Shared reading provides a bridge between read-aloud, where the teacher does the reading and provides the maximum amount of support for the students, and guided and independent reading, where the students are the readers. Books read several times can be read independently by the students at another time.

Shared reading is another context where words can be explained and enjoyed. Poetry Out Loud and Readers Theater are both contexts in which language can be enjoyed for the sake of its sound and rhythm, its power to create feeling and mood. In this section we offer some suggestions for bringing greater word awareness to the classroom through shared reading activities. All of us enjoyed reading out loud with our classes and expected that our students would be enthusiastic performers of out-loud reading.

The benefits of doing shared reading with a class are many. Shared reading provides an opportunity for direct instruction about word solving and decoding, about comprehension and meaning, and about specific vocabulary and word consciousness. Shared reading builds class culture as the repertoire of stories, poems, and plays, read out loud together, becomes part of the memory bank of the class. We include Readers Theater in this category, as Readers Theater is rehearsed and all the students are involved in the use of a common script, though not all are reading the same part. Shared reading also supports those students who are more hesitant in their reading as they read along with more fluent students. This support increases confidence, fluency, and prosody, especially if the reading is repeated. Since we are always trying to make the link between what is read and what the students might write, this becomes an opportunity to ask the question, How might this text help us learn about words we can use in our writing? We especially found it a useful strategy during poetry units.

SHARED READING USING A POEM

Poetry can be presented to the class on chart paper on a chart stand, or on an overhead using a projector. We all feel that there is no greater fun in the classroom than whole-group shared reading of poetry, and it is not a time-consuming activity. As we all read together, we can play with the volume, the speed, the intonation, and the expressiveness of the reading. Students can take parts and read in pairs or individually. The repeated reading of poems builds a class repertoire of favorite and meaningful verse. Poetry read aloud helps students with articulation, expression, and comprehension as well as fluency, and it most definitely helps in the writing program as students learn from poets how to say important things with few words.

Vocabulary learning can be a large part of shared poetry reading. As poems are read together, Gifts of Words will jump out at the class. The class word bank will fill with phrases that the class enjoyed.

Introducing a Poem for Shared Reading

Display the poem and ask the students to look at it carefully. Read it out loud to the class, using a pointer to track the print. After reading, ask the students to pick out any difficult or challenging words as well as any words they don't understand or are curious about. Record these words and discuss them with the class. Alternatively, you can distribute photocopies of poems and give students highlighters or crayons. They should read each poem silently and highlight those words that are unusual or challenging, words they don't know, or words that intrigue them. Before you begin reading out loud, the class discusses those words that were chosen, and you record the words that the students highlighted. This way, the difficulties are smoothed out before the reading. Here, you can point out words that are related morphologically, words that may have multiple meanings, and words that present a new shade of meaning for a more common word.

Then involve the class in discussion about the poem and ask for their personal responses: What did they like? What part of the poem is interesting, fun, or unusual? Do they have any personal connections to make? Sometimes this is done as a partner activity. Ask them to think-pair-share before reporting to the whole class. Sometimes it is enough just to think-pair-share without having a whole-class discussion.

At first we all read together, and after one reading we begin to think of ways to make the reading more interesting. When we divide the text into sections, different students can read different parts. We look for places where it would be good to read slower or faster. We then look for opportunities for crescendo or diminuendo and begin to orchestrate the reading.

Classroom Snapshot

Many different poems, such as the one given below, are written to be read aloud by two voices—sometimes alternating, sometimes simultaneously. A wonderful source for such poems is the collection entitled *Joyful Noise: Poems for Two Voices*, by Paul Fleischman (1988). Judy and Jan wrote the following poem to be read aloud by two groups of students.

Seaside Senses (to be read in two voices)

Voice #1	Voice #2
Crabs squirming beneath the sand	
	Slurp, slip, squishing in the tide
Children challenge foamy waves	
	Splashing, squealing as they run
Sea gulls swerving overhead	
	Squawking, screeching as they swirl

All: Oh the sounds, the symphony of sounds in summer

Kelp mounds sprawling on the beach	
	Silky ropes of stinky pods
Sunscreen wafting from the towels	
	Sprays and spreads of coconut
Bonfires blaze in dusky night	
	Wood smoke streams into the sky

All: Oh the smell, the salty smell of summer

Quickly running 'cross the beach	
	Sizzling sprint in scorching sun
Pools form in clefts and cavities	
	Submerged, slimy spas of life
Pulling tide against your shins	
	Sinking, sliding, shifting sand

All: Oh the feel, the sweet sensation of summer

The class begins by reading the poem and noting words they want to discuss on sticky notes, which they attach to the book. They are then given these questions to discuss with a friend:

- Have you ever gone to an ocean beach in the summer?
- What pictures do you see in your mind as you read this poem?
- How is it similar or different from what you have experienced?
- Which words are unusual or difficult? Are there any words that you need to look up or have explained?

Through discussion, the class clarifies the meaning of words like *swerving, wafting, blaze, cleft, cavities,* and *submerged.* The fact that there are so many vivid verbs in the poem will probably lead to a discussion about slight differences in meaning. How are *squawking* and *screeching* similar and different? The imagery of the shoreline may remind them of their own experiences on a beach, so a discussion around their memories and the poem will help solidify the meaning of the words.

Next, the class is divided into two groups and attempts an initial reading of the poem in two parts. Voice #2 echoes Voice #1, and everyone joins together to read the sentences marked "All." This poem is formatted for easy choral reading. However, when Jan's class read "Whirligig Beetles" by Paul Fleischman (1988), it became immediately clear that there were pauses for both groups that had to be observed, and this made the reading trickier than it seemed at first. The discovery of the rhythm of the verse helped, and on the second reading there was a definite exaggeration of emphasis, producing a rhythmic drone with a circular feel to it.

The class then discussed ways to make the reading more dramatic and interesting. The difference in sound and cadence were discussed between the flowing section where the language is *whirling* and *weaving,* compared with staccato *arcs, ovals,* and *loops* in a subsequent section. Consequently, certain parts were read in a louder and more affirmative manner. Finally, after several rehearsals, students were ready to perform for an audience of younger children.

When the class reviews the poems, they look for those words and phrases they like the best. These are added to their wordcatchers, and the ones voted as their favorites go into the class word bank.

SHARED READING USING AN ANTHOLOGY

Many classroom reading programs are supported by the resources chosen by the school or district. In many cases an anthology is used, and students all read the same stories, poems, and essays as part of the language arts program. Traditionally, the teacher's guide will select several vocabulary items for study. Students may look up the chosen words in their dictionaries, and at the end of the reading, answer questions about the passage that include focus items that pick up on the meaning and use of these vocabulary words.

In our classrooms we turned this method around to fit in with our philosophy of student ownership and engagement. We asked the students to choose words from the reading that were interesting, exciting, or unusual. They were to highlight, using sticky notes, those words that gave them pause for thought. After everyone had skimmed the text and chosen their Gifts of Words or "problem words," these were shared and written on the board. Any words that seemed problematic were discussed. Dictionaries were used on occasion to find definitions, and the meaning most appropriate for the text was chosen.

Typically, when looking for Gifts of Words, students begin by finding similes and idioms. But with time and experience, the list broadens to include many more ways of using language. The following examples are from *Solomon's Tree* by Andrea Spalding:

Descriptive phrases (they paint a picture using strong nouns and adjectives): *Solomon gazed in astonishment at the fragment of woven lichen clinging to a forked twig and marveled at the tiny eggs, smaller than his fingernail.*

Emotional phrases (you can feel what the character is feeling): *"My tree," sobbed Solomon the next morning. He ran through the rain and hugged the fallen trunk.*

Action phrases (you can see and hear the action): *The chainsaw whirred and sawdust flew as Uncle made the first cuts.*

Metaphors (one idea used to describe another): *A brand-new butterfly unfolded its wings and danced away on the breeze.*

Alliteration (sounds, especially repeating initial consonants, used to create an effect): *The old maple…writhed and wriggled…*

Personification (the inanimate described as if it were alive): *The maple gave a last despairing cry, crashed over the woodshed, and fell silent.*

Idioms (well-known sayings and ways of expressing ideas): *The wood sprang to life.*

Sensory imagery (reference to sight, sound, touch, taste, and smell): *Solomon remembered the sweet spring smell of sap and the pungent fall odor of crushed leaves.*

Strong verbs (unusual and effective choices of verbs): *Its branches cradled his body.*

This work is sometimes done with partners. Taking turns to read a paragraph aloud to a partner, students work their way through a passage. One student reads the first paragraph while the other listens. Then they reverse roles. Together they choose those words that they both think should be discussed by the class. After this word work, the class discusses the text and clarifies any word meanings that are still unclear. This method works very well for informational text and for stories. A variation for poetry entails discussion as partners and then choral reading as a class.

As a result of this activity while reading the anthology, the Bank of Powerful Language is continually updated. The new phrases and words maintain high interest in the word bank and students are ready to withdraw words and phrases from the bank when they need them during writing workshop.

Thoughts to Ponder

It is during read-alouds and shared reading that we model what "good" readers do. Our students love to be read to and become eager participants in reading together. While reading, share your own struggles over words—strategies you use when you lose your place, when you forget what happened, or when you read a passage you didn't quite get. We have found that reluctant readers believe that good readers know all the words, always know what is happening, and never make any kind of mistakes. Here is the opportunity to model and share every reader's struggle.

Picture books are priceless in offering models of powerful language. Extended reading of novels, poetry, nonfiction, and snippets that catch our eyes and ears is also part of our repertoire. The texts we share in these contexts are the foundation for our writing program.

——— ❊ ———

Chapter 5

Learning Vocabulary Through Reading Novels Together

Before I read just for the story.
I've never noticed Gift of Words before, but now I sure do.
—Tyson, grade 4

By fourth grade our students are, by and large, independent readers, and this independence grows during the middle school years. Many students can pick up a novel and recognize whether or not it is too easy, too hard, or just right for them to read. They typically have begun to develop a taste for reading, knowing the sorts of books they will enjoy. They devour reading series by a particular author and read their way through favorite genres—adventure, mystery, animal stories, and fantasy. They like nonfiction as well as fiction. We allow our students to choose their own books for independent reading, knowing that we are helping them build confidence and stamina by reading books they feel motivated to read.

Our classrooms are rich in books and reading materials. By making use of school and local libraries, purchasing through book clubs and at garage sales, and fund-raising at the school level, we have stocked our classrooms with novels, picture books, magazines, and nonfiction books of all types. These books represent a range of reading difficulty and interests, and are used to promote recreational reading as a lifelong habit.

Every day time is set aside for independent reading, and reading is high on the list of homework expectations for our students. We encourage parents to read aloud to their children, to share books together whatever the age of the students, and to assist students in finding time to read independently at home. We recognize that all parents are not fluent English readers, so we send home books on tape and enlist siblings as reading partners. We realize that parental support comes in many different forms.

Several strategies are used to promote the quantity of independent reading that is completed. In reading logs, students record titles and comments about each book. Weekly sharing circles allow students to talk about books that appeal to them. The number of titles read in the class is updated weekly, with the score creeping into the thousands as the term progresses. All genres of reading material are deemed acceptable, including comic books. However, reading records and teacher-student conferences help us monitor the types of books being selected and help students make a variety of choices. Jan developed a reading record wheel that tracks books by genre (see Figure 5-1). She found that this is an effective visual aid to help guide students into additional genres and to help students monitor their own reading experiences.

As the students read independently, the classroom becomes filled with talk about books and authors. This promotes the type of reading culture that we all agree is essential to our overall goals. Time for independent reading is one piece of a complex instructional puzzle that includes teaching, talk, and the selection of texts. Richard Allington (2002) argues that students need more time to read in the classroom by saying, "If we want to increase substantially the amount of reading that children do (and I would argue that this is one absolutely crucial step toward enhancing reading proficiency), it is important to give children books they *can* read and choices regarding which books they *will* read" (p. 746, original italics).

In our classrooms we all conduct individual reading conferences, and these focus on the students' responses to text they have already read. By talking to each student, we check in with their reading choices and their enjoyment of books.

However, we also want to build a community of readers, and when everyone is reading something different, this is hard to achieve. We need some common texts in the classroom that everyone can discuss and through which we focus on and enhance comprehension strategies. Reading aloud to students, regardless of their grade level, is a springboard for this discussion. Reading a novel aloud and modeling our own wonder at how writers craft their choice of

Circle Reading Log

Name _____

Grade _____

Keep this log as a record of your independent reading. On the circle graph below you will see many types of texts listed. When you have finished reading a book or a magazine, just color one section of the chart that shows what kind of text it is. For example, if you have read a book about hockey, you would color one segment of the sports section of the circle graph.

As time passes, try to read widely around the wheel and experience many subjects and types of reading. If you are not sure where to place a text, just ask your teacher or teacher-librarian.

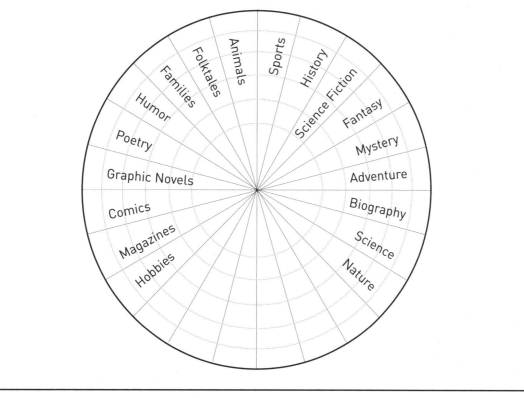

Fig. 5-1: Reading Record Wheel

words goes a long way to inspire our students to both read more and write with more enthusiasm. Finding Gifts of Words together helps to build a class culture. Without this focus on words, our students' reading is like watching a black-and-white film; being conscious of the wonder of words is like stepping into the Land of Oz, with its dizzying array of color. Everything comes alive: setting, characters, and the main events.

But we wanted to go further. We wanted students to be word conscious in their own reading, so we introduced group novels and literature circles to create the meaningful discussions that model the lives of real adult readers.

At first, we wondered whether we could achieve this "real world" reading in the classroom. To investigate this premise, our teacher research group decided to try a literature group discussion on our own, with the novel *A Taste for Death* by P. D. James. This is a mystery set in England where a murder takes place in a church. Our "assignment" was to examine ourselves as readers. In other words, what could we learn about reading that would inform our teaching of reading? Try this sometime—it was quite revealing. At no time, for instance, did anyone in the group have a burning desire to stop and write a summary, do a plot profile, draw a story map, or answer comprehension questions.

The following are some of our insights:

- Our prior knowledge of England and religion made a significant difference in our ability to follow this somewhat complicated story.
- We all reread parts of the story as a strategy to clarify our reading.
- We all had our favorite parts and parts we found difficult. It was only through our discussion that certain parts of the book were clarified.
- We chose Gifts of Words and there were certain phrases that everyone agreed were models of excellent word use.
- When we came across words we didn't know, we all skipped them at times. If the meaning of the word was important to our understanding, we'd stop and figure it out from context and occasionally look up meanings in the dictionary. For those members who did not have the background knowledge of religion, looking up a religious word in the dictionary really didn't help.
- Each of us agreed that "getting into the story" was essential. "Getting into the story" occurred only when we had extended time to read. Two of us with young children stayed up late into the night, since reading in 15-minute segments was so unsatisfactory.

The question of importance is, How did this experience make us better reading teachers? How did it inform us so that reading could be made more meaningful for our students? We realized that the discussion before, during, and after reading was the key to our better understanding. If this was true for our group, could this be true for our students? We examined the activities that we had been using in our classrooms. After-reading responses such as creating profiles, storyboards, new book covers, Wanted posters, and character passports meant that students spent one to two weeks reading and four to five weeks completing activities that often had drawing and coloring as their main focus.

Literature circles, with their focus on extended discussion, seemed to be the answer. We read Harvey Daniels's *Literature Circles: Voice and Choice in the Student-Centered Classroom* (1994) and *Grand Conversations* by Ralph Petersen and Maryann Eeds (1990). However, as we began to implement literature circles in our various classrooms, we built word-conscious activities into the discussion frames.

Book selections to get started!

In this chapter, we present three approaches to reading a novel together with a class set of books—*The Half-a-Moon Inn* by Paul Fleischman, *The Bone Collector's Son* by Paul Yee, and *The Sky Is Falling* by Kit Pearson. Through these three whole-class experiences we guide students toward independence in literature circle groups. All three approaches are stepping stones toward the students' being able to choose their own books, write meaningful responses in their reading journals, meet in groups to share these responses, and deepen their appreciation and understanding of the novel. All three approaches emphasize word consciousness. You will, of course, select books that are meaningful for you and your students. These units of study are intended as exemplars.

Exploring the Whole-Class Novel Study

A whole-class novel study presents both challenges and advantages. The book you choose, like the three presented here, should be easily accessible to most of the students in your class with scaffolding. With a wide range of students, this can be difficult, although we've found that providing less proficient readers with books on tape, or enlisting the support of parents who might read aloud at home, is worthwhile. The advantage of a class novel study is that it is a step toward independence between reading aloud, where the teacher does all the work, and independent reading. It is an excellent way to model reading strategies, create a common bond through text, and provide reading opportunities.

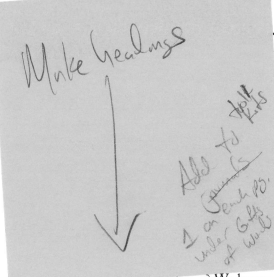

Make headings

Add to notes

1 on each p.s. under Gifts of Words

...EISCHMAN

...pelling story line and interesting, unusual char-
..., and a mystical innkeeper—that all age groups
...itely created with words that students embrace.

...e sticky notes to mark instances of powerful
...ese and talk about why each word or phrase
...their favorite Gifts of Words to deposit into
...developing reasons for choosing Gifts of
...eason for inclusion in the bank. What was
...e word or the phrase? We began a list of characteristics that identify a Gift of
Words. Here are some examples of Gifts of Words and the reasons they were selected.

THE AUTHOR MAKES YOU FEEL WHAT THE CHARACTERS ARE FEELING *Emotions & feelings character*

He felt as restless as a chipmunk on the first day of spring, for it was but once a month that they
left the seacoast behind them and wound their way through the forest to Craftsbury, where
all the world seemed together on market day (p. 1).

"I like this Gift of Words because I know what it feels like to be restless as a chipmunk.
Aaron is excited to be going to market and he's all jumpy." (Robbie, grade 5)

The woods are full of wolf packs and bears, and a-crawling with brigands like a corpse full of
maggots (p. 5).

"This Gift of Words makes my skin creep. The woods are very dangerous with brigands and
wolves. It's a good Gift of Words because you can feel the danger." (Charlotte, grade 5)

THE IMAGE IS VERY VISUAL: YOU CAN REALLY IMAGINE IT IN YOUR MIND'S EYE *Setting*

For there's no town to be reached but by traveling inland, where the roads wriggle about the for-
est like a family of snakes, broad and fine as the king's highway one minute and dwindling
down to rabbit runs the next (p. 5).

"This is a good Gift of Words because you can imagine the roads twisting and turning
through the forest." (Roberto, grade 5)

He stared at the wall across the room, and seemed to see it almost imperceptibly bulge and sink,
like the skin over a heart (p. 10).

"I liked this because I could see the walls moving." (Alexander, grade 5)

THE WORDS SOUND GOOD TOGETHER (ONOMATOPOEIA AND ALLITERATION)

The house felt as lifeless as a tomb, and he longed to hear the sound of his mother spinning, or of her softly singing while she wove (p. 10).

"The sounds of the singing and the spinning are all *s* sounds so you can hear the sound."
(Carly, grade 5)

Webbing

Working in small groups, students put the words *powerful language* in the center of a large piece of chart paper. They look for words and phrases that they might find useful in their own writing and record these on a web (see the example in Figure 5-2). This process can be focused on words that describe settings or characters.

Illustrations

Each student chooses his or her favorite Gift of Words from the novel and illustrates it. The drawing helps the child visualize the images that the words have created in the mind's eye. It makes concrete what might be a transitory or fleeting image, and brings the word's meaning sharply into focus. Drawing a picture of a Gift of Words can be done all year long, at any time, to enhance comprehension. It aids visualization, sharpens the imagination, and can be used during read-aloud time as well as during independent reading.

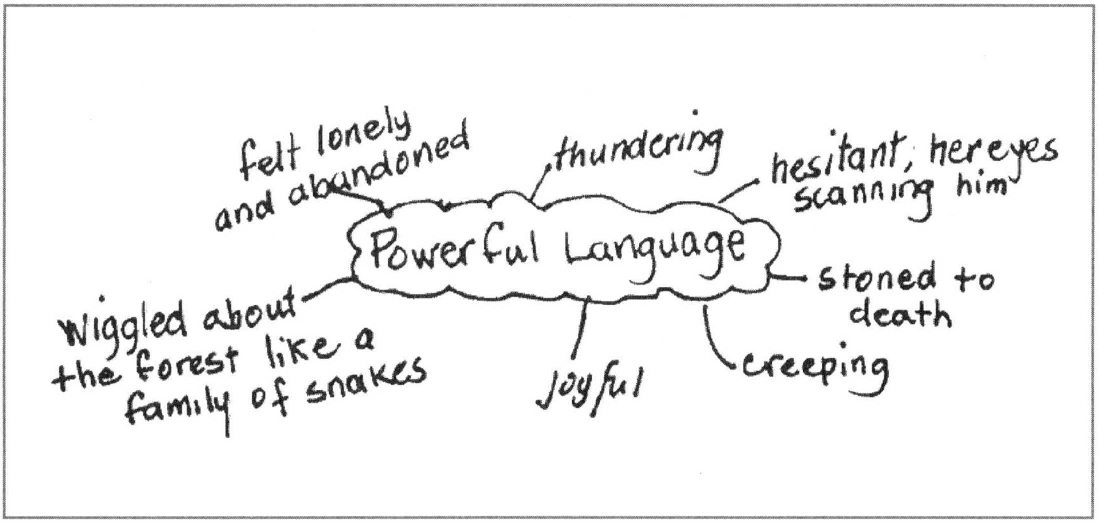

Fig. 5-2: Gifts of Words From *The Half-a-Moon Inn*

Perspective Journal

This is a written response completed after the novel is finished. The students imagine themselves to be one of the main characters, and from that perspective they retell the story. They draw on the word bank because by now it is full of words and phrases that relate to the characters. They have discussed character traits as they read the book. They may have dramatized a scene, bringing characters to life. These activities are the necessary scaffolds that enable them to take on the persona of a character in their writing. By the end of the novel, each student should be very familiar with each character.

Before they write, it is helpful to show them what a first-person narrative looks like, perhaps sharing a sample of what a journal might sound like. Even our most reluctant writers can produce a thoughtful journal entry given the scaffolding and access to the word bank. One of the wonderful advantages of having the bank is that reluctant writers have a way of "improv-

---

Aaron's Diary

Entry #1

My Mom has just wandered off in the *forest of thieves and marauders*. It is Monday. 5:00 p.m. and I have just finished making dinner for myself. My Mom was supposed to have been back and she is not here. *A chill ran up my spine. A coldness filled the air.* Just the feeling that she is out there alone in the forest that is *crawling with brigands like a corpse full of maggots* makes me scared. Just the feeling gives me the creepy crawlies.

Entry #2

I *trudged up the endless road* with my sack of food. I ate after an hour or two. I stopped once and looked around where the *road twisted like an eel*. I couldn't even see the ocean! It kept *snowing hour on end* and my feet hurt. I broke some twigs off a tree and made a fire. Suddenly a man appeared, *burly and dressed as raggedly as a scarecrow*. He was a ragman and he pointed a pistol right at me.

Entry #3

Later we came to a motel called The Half-a-Moon Inn. I knocked at the door and a *bear sized woman wrapped in shawls like a mummy* opened it. She let me in but in a nasty way. She made me light the fires and told me to make the *"flames crack like whips."* I tried to escape but Ms. Grackle hit me with a willow stick.

---

ing" their work. Initially these students may misuse the Gift of Words, but we've learned to be patient, celebrate their approximations, and try to gently nudge them in a more effective direction, keeping in mind their zone of proximal development. The box "Aaron's Diary" shows sample diary entries written from the perspective of the main character, Aaron. Gifts of Words are italicized.

Another example of a perspective journal entry is given for *I Am David* in Chapter 4 (page 53). We have found that it is valuable to use the same activities for different books with different interaction structures. The similarity and repetition of these activities helps solidify students' understanding and competence.

THE BONE COLLECTOR'S SON BY PAUL YEE

This novel is set in Vancouver in the early 1900s and concerns the life of a young boy, Bing-wing Chan, who lives with his father and uncle in a communal dwelling in Vancouver's Chinatown. The book is particularly good as a novel study because both period and setting are unfamiliar. Students have little prior knowledge and need to work at identifying with the characters and plot through understanding some difficult vocabulary.

Cover Story

This is a prereading strategy that engages students and draws upon their ability to make connections and access background knowledge. Students are engaged in actively constructing meaning.

Make an overhead transparency and photocopies of the cover for the students. Consider blacking out the title, to make the work focus more closely on the picture. Model your thinking aloud by showing the overhead as you examine the details in the picture. For example: "I can see two people. One looks like a boy. He is holding a basket of bones and there are bones on the ground. I think they must be in a graveyard. I wonder what they are doing there with the bones?" As you talk, label the picture with words and phrases that reflect your inferences, comments, and questions. Ask the students to turn to their own copies of the cover and continue to make observations, labeling the drawing with words and phases. Ask the students to share their ideas with partners before asking the whole class to discuss what they have learned from the cover. Finally, ask students to read the blurb on the back of the book:

> *This ghost story is set in the year 1907 in Vancouver, British Columbia. Fourteen-year-old*
> *Bing-wing Chan resents his father, not only because the man gambles away all their*

money, but also because he now forces Bing to join him in his gruesome job. Ba is the bone collector, the one who digs up skeletons of deceased Chinese so that they can be sent home to China for permanent burial. Sinister things start happening soon after Bing accompanies his father to the graveyard.

Discuss what this information adds to their knowledge of the book. As a result of these discussions, the students should know that this is a historical novel, set in Vancouver in 1907; that it concerns Bing-wing Chan and his father; and that they are engaged in collecting the bones of the deceased Chinese for repatriation. It is a ghost story with a sinister undercurrent.

Making Connections: Using Reading Response Logs (Chapters 1–4)

Students read Chapters 1–4 with pen in hand. They use reading response logs to record and hold their thinking while they read. These logs provide a place to write in response to a text. The writing then becomes a text for talk in their discussion with others. Students learn that there are many different ways to understand and respond to a text. Reading response logs slow down the reading process and cause students to seek deeper understandings of plot, character, setting, and author's point of view. This strategy helps them enter the world of the text, taking new perspectives. Thinking from the perspective of personal connections is one of the roles we want our students to learn.

Begin by marking the first chapter with four stopping points. Give sticky notes to the students to mark the four places in their books. Read aloud up to the first stopping point. Students follow along in their copies of the book. Model the process of making connections by thinking aloud your connections. These can be personal connections (text to self), connections to general knowledge (text to world), or connections to other texts (text to text) (Harvey & Goudvis, 2000).

For example, on pages 3–4, the text reads: "Most of the graves were crowned with elaborate granite and marble headstones." The teacher stopped after reading this sentence and said, "When I read about Bing and his father in the graveyard, I remember the graveyard where my grandmother is buried. The graves are in rows, each with a rectangle of garden around them. Many of them have chips of colored marble scattered over the surface. Some of the graves are neglected and forgotten because they have been there for over a hundred years, and no one remembers the people buried there. This makes me think about the way we remember the dead and what they mean to us. I have a question: I wonder why the Chinese men wanted to be buried back in China and not stay in the Canadian graveyard."

Tell students to read on to the second stopping point. Tell them they are to write about thoughts that come to mind at that place in the text. What ideas do they have? What does the text make them think about or remember? Can they connect the text to something they already know? What unanswered questions do they have? There are no right answers to be found; it is important for the students to know that their ideas are valuable.

Stop to discuss as a class the connections that are made. Begin to draw out the big ideas of the chapter. (Bing is afraid of ghosts; his father bullies his son; the Chinese and the white people follow different customs; the white people are not friendly toward the Chinese; Bing experiences discrimination at school.)

Set the task of reading Chapters 2–4 and ask the students to stop three times, once in each chapter. After stopping, they write a paragraph in which they make connections to what they read in their chapter. Share the connections made in Chapters 1–4 before reading further.

Using Contextual Clues and Making Clue Cards (Chapter 5)

Challenging or interesting vocabulary becomes the focus of this section of the reading. Students are taught to use contextual information to work out the meaning of unknown words. This focus on words helps develop word consciousness and helps students to self-monitor their understanding.

Model the process of stopping to review words—for example, *water closet* on page 55: *A fist pounded the door and Big Ming called out, "Hey Little One, it's your turn to use the water closet!"*

You might say: "If I do not know what a water closet is, I must use what I know about life and look around in the sentences before and after for clues. Bing has just woken up and is lying in bed. He jumps up because it is his turn to use the water closet. This is something he must wait in line for. And it has to do with *water* and a *closet*. A bathroom is small like a closet and has water in it. I guess it might be the bathroom that is shared with all the men who live at Uncle Won's."

Students read Chapter 5 with pencil in hand. As they come to a word they don't know, they write out the word and look for clues in the sentences around it. The following words may be challenging: *muzzle, aching, shoveled, merchant, hoodlums, cudgel, persecution, martial arts, sauntered, nagging.*

If a word can't be guessed from the context and word parts, students then use the dictionary to find the meaning or refer to a search engine for a definition. ("What is a water closet?" reveals the following definition: "A plumbing fixture having a water-containing receptor which receives liquid and solid body waste and, upon actuation (flushing), conveys waste through a trapway into a gravity drainage system.")

Finally, students make a set of clues for the new words. They write a clue on one side of a card (e.g., a word meaning "flush toilet"). On the other side of the card they write the answer (water closet). Students challenge their friends to read the definitions and guess the words.

Another suggestion is to collect the cards and transfer them to "I have/Who has" cards to play Ricochet (see Chapter 3). You or the students can record other words throughout the other chapters to add to the Ricochet set of cards. Character names, places, events, and opinions from the novel can be used for the Ricochet cards as well.

Finding Gifts of Words (Chapter 6)

This activity extends the focus on words to consider the author's word choice and the effectiveness of word use. It highlights language and makes students conscious of the power of words to convey ideas. It also teaches how to record quotations. Our students are familiar with the concept of Gifts of Words and here they practice finding them and deciding on the reasons for their choices.

Model the process of highlighting interesting, striking, or powerful uses of language, such as this sentence from page 60: *Lee Dat bounced a knuckle off Bing's forehead.* You might say, "*Bounced* is a good word to use here because it indicates that Lee is being playful with Bing. He is not being cruel and hitting him with his knuckles. He is joking with him about ghosts and being scared."

Or you might choose this sentence—*Nearby trees were so tall and thick it would take six men with their arms outstretched to encircle their trunks* (p. 61)—and comment, "This is a Gift of Words, because the image of six men holding hands around a tree trunk really helps you to imagine how enormous the trees were."

Establish criteria for describing Gifts of Words. Strong responses give details and explanations. Weak responses are too general and lack detail.

Reading Chapter 6 with pencil in hand, students write out their Gifts of Words, record the sentence in which the words or phrases occur, and note the page number. They underline each Gift of Words. Then, they write one or two sentences that explain why they believe this to be a Gift of Words. Each student should find at least four Gifts of Words. They then share their Gifts of Words and write out their favorites on long strips of paper to post on the bulletin board. These phrases are added to the Bank of Powerful Language. This activity practices the role of word hunter, which later they will use in literature circles.

Summarizing the Plot (Chapters 7, 8, 9, and 10)

Synthesizing the main ideas and finding the support for those ideas in the details is an important reading skill. In this activity, students will read four chapters, then review the main events of these chapters as a whole, and retell them in six episodes, using drawing.

Talk with the students about finding the main idea of a piece of text. Model this by referring to Chapter 6. What happened in Chapter 6? What is the big picture emerging from that chapter? (Bing begins his work as a houseboy at Bulldog Bentley's home in Fairview. He is shown the house by the housekeeper, Mrs. Moore, and learns about his work. He also learns that the house is for sale, that Bulldog is setting off on a boxing tour, and that Mr. Bentley Sr. died in the house. Bing hears a man coughing in Mr. Bentley's room and concludes that his ghost is still there.)

Tell the students that they are going to read the next four chapters and afterward, draw six sketches that tell the main ideas that emerge. Fold a piece of paper into six boxes; students will put one sketch in each box. The sketches will represent the six most important things that the students think happened in those chapters. One sentence may accompany each picture. They will then share their ideas orally with partners and as a class. This activity foreshadows the role of discussion director that we want them to use in literature circles.

Predicting the End

Stopping at this point to predict the end of the story focuses attention on the action and the possible outcomes. It engages students in actively seeking the meaning and being involved in the story. Predicting is one of the thinking skills that discussion directors will be asked to do in literature circles.

Before reading the final chapters (11–17), ask the students to take out their reading logs and write. They should describe what they think will happen to Bing, to his father, to Mrs. Bentley, and to the bones of Shrum. They need to consider in detail all the threads of the plot as they come together at this stage. How will this story end? They can pose questions and hypothesize possible answers. After reading, ask students to review their predictions. What worked out as they thought it would? What surprises were there?

Final Discussion

The final discussion pulls all the threads together. Students jointly construct an opinion of the book—what it has taught us and how well it engaged our attention. Then engage the students in a reflective conversation about what they learned from the book.

- What have they discovered about the life of the early Chinese immigrants to Vancouver?
- What have they learned about the race riots of 1907 by reading the book?
- What have they learned about the way some of the white people behaved toward the Chinese immigrants?
- Would they have liked the life of a boy like Bing? How was his life different from their lives? What was good about his life? What was hard about his life?
- Do they believe in ghosts as a result of reading this book? Are there such things as ghosts?
- What questions would the class have for Paul Lee if they were to meet him?
- Which new words have they learned? What was their favorite Gift of Words?

Evaluation

Choose one of the following assignments to evaluate students' comprehension and appreciation of the novel.

- Write a review of the book recommending it to others. Explain in a persuasive essay style why people should read the book. Use descriptive language to refer to characters, plot, and setting. Mention the feelings evoked by the book.
- Create a "container for a character" for Bing. In a small box, place tiny objects that symbolize what you know about the character of Bing and what happened to him in the story. Write an explanation of why you chose the objects and how they represent the character. Use powerful language in your description.
- Write a perspective journal from the point of view of Bing and tell the story in his own words. Use Gifts of Words from the novel if you wish.

THE SKY IS FALLING BY KIT PEARSON: MOVING TOWARD INDEPENDENCE

Once students are comfortable with the more structured class novel studies and potential roles to play, we move into literature circles that offer greater freedom of choice. Students read the novel in sections, write responses, and talk about what they read, using their writing as "text for talk" (Kooy & Wells, 1996). They meet in groups of four, maintaining the same group for the duration of the novel. The novel is divided into readable sections, and students respond by taking on one of four roles based on those described by Harvey Daniels (1994) and described in depth in the following text. They write their response, bring it to the group, and engage in group discussion. Note that our word hunter role focuses to a greater extent on author's word choice than on definitions. An assignment for evaluation concludes the unit.

We like Harvey Daniels's roles for this age group as we really see the benefit of breaking down the task of responding to text into manageable chunks. It is too overwhelming to be asked to write anything you can think of—and the roles help structure not only the writing but also the discussion. This is valuable scaffolding for young learners.

The actual reading and writing can be done during silent reading time or at home. For the

---

The Sky Is Falling by **Kit Pearson**

You will be reading this novel together with your classmates during the next six weeks. You are required to do the following assignments:

- Read the chapters assigned by the dates posted on the homework board. You can read in school and at home, but you *must have your book and your journal in school for discussions*. Some chapters may be read aloud in class by your teacher.
- Keep a reading journal with entries written chapter by chapter and be ready to share in discussions on the dates posted. You will have different roles for different chapters. The roles are:
    Discussion directors
    Connectors
    Word hunters
    Friends of the characters
- Bring your reading journal to class and be ready to talk about the chapters with your group. You will meet with people who have had different roles. You are responsible for your role in the group.

Determine how you will do a good job in this unit:

- Be ready on time with the chapter read.
- Do your responses in time for the discussion.
- Bring your journal to class with the entries up-to-date.
- Be prepared to talk in your group.

---

slow or reluctant reader, 20 to 30 minutes a day is not enough time to get into the novel. They need prolonged periods for reading, just as our vocabulary group discovered for ourselves. Maybe reluctant readers are those who have never "gotten into" a story. Perhaps most adults would have a hard time reading if their only reading time was 30 minutes of USSR (uninterrupted sustained silent reading) or DEAR (drop everything and read) time! For our most challenged readers, a tape recording of the book under consideration is a great help, as is the support of parents or siblings who might read aloud at home, or other professionals in the school who support the learner. To get the process going, the instructions shown in the box on page 79 are given to students.

The four roles—discussion director, word hunter, connector, and friends of the characters—are described in the box "Guidelines for Keeping Your Reading Journal." This information is both given to the students on a handout and posted on a chart on the wall.

The Literature Circles Process

Once the roles have been introduced, we post descriptions of the roles on the wall and create laminated cards with the roles that can sit on the tables during discussions. To begin the role assignments, list the roles on the chalkboard and have the students sign up for one of the four roles. There will be one of each role in every group; your knowledge of the students will help you organize them into groups of four. It is important to have heterogeneous groups with capable readers and to distribute those with good small-group skills evenly throughout the class. One way to sort the students is to put each role on a different color card and transfer the names of students from the sign-up sheet onto the cards. Then divide the students into equally matched groups representing all four roles, using the cards.

Set the amount of reading to be done by a due date. Using their reader response journals, each child reads and responds following the guidelines for writing and with the perspective of the particular role for which he or she has signed up.

After the first few chapters, students meet in their small groups of four students to discuss the book so far. All members of the group take turns to read aloud their written entry from their journal and then discuss the issues arising. Whole-class discussions bring everyone's "big ideas" together as they share the comments that have come up in the small groups.

Set the target amount of reading to be done by the next due date and change roles. Continue in this way until the novel is finished and everyone has held each role at least once.

Guidelines for Keeping Your Reading Journal

At the end of each chapter, take out your journal and write! You will have one of the following roles.

Discussion Director

Write about one or more of the following things:

- Any questions you have about what is happening in the story
- Any predictions you might have
- Anything of importance that you think your group should discuss about this chapter

Connector

- Write about any connections you make between the events in the book and your own experience.
- Discuss whether you have ever felt like the character in the book.
- Write about a time you were placed in a situation similar to the one faced by the character in the book.
- Address how you feel about what's happening: Does it puzzle you? Make you mad, sad, or happy?
- See if you can make a text-to-text or text-to-world connection.

Word Hunter

- Write any words or phrases that jump out at you as evidence of the writer's craft or seem to you to be a Gift of Words. Include the page number on which the words occur so that you may find them easily.
- Describe what it is you like about these words. Why are they special? Remember to give detailed reasons for your choices.
- Write three or four words that puzzle you or are difficult for you. Describe how you found the meaning of these words and what problem-solving strategy you used.

Friend of the Characters

Write about the characters in the novel:

- What is happening to them?
- How are they feeling?
- What sort of people are they?
- Why do they behave the way they do?

Examples From the Classroom

Using this process, Jan's students read and talked their way through the novel. Here are some examples of the writing that was produced in their reading journals. Sabrina was a friend of the characters for the first section. She wrote:

> Norah found a Nazi warplane that had been shot down. Norah knows that she is going to be sent away to Canada with her brother Gavin but she doesn't want to go. I think they feel happy when they find the plane and curious. I think they are very nice people. (One of those everyday humorous people). I think they behave the way they did because they probably have a mix of attitudes from their parents and they get curious like all other people. I would like Norah to be my friend because she is very brave and courageous.

Alexa, as another friend of the characters, wrote:

> I think Norah is kind of excited about the war. She does not want to come to Canada. She has one brother; a mum and I think she has a dad too. We have not heard much about him or the brother. I think she is taking her problem maturely. The story takes place during W.W.II in England. The fighting is coming closer to them. Norah and her friends want to help. She is very brave and courageous.

Both Sabrina and Alexa show that they have grasped the essential ordinariness and yet the feistiness of Norah Stokes. Very much the tomboy, Norah races around Ringden doing her bit for the war effort by spotting German aircraft. The impending crisis of evacuation to Canada is hinted at in the first chapter, but Norah is unwilling to believe that her parents would ever send her away. As friends of the characters, these students not only describe some of the events of the chapters, but also begin to think about characterization and feelings.

Jacob, a connector for this section, wrote:

> I think Norah is scared and curious because she's leaving her family and is going to a whole different country, also a different continent. She also has to go on a boat all the way to Canada just with her brother. I felt scared and curious when I was six years old and had to go to Calgary with my parents because I didn't really know where we were going. I was also curious because I was going somewhere new but also kind of scared and excited at the same time.

Jacob is able to express the ambiguity of feeling that accompanies change, relating it to a remembered event. At the same time, he tells us about the feelings of Norah and gives reasons she feels the way she does. Connectors and friends of the characters often talk about the same things but with a different slant.

Word hunters created lists of words and phrases. Here are some examples of Gifts of Words chosen by Victor from the novel:

Wave upon wave glistening against the blue sky. "I like it because it brings you into the story."

The trees blazed like a fire. "I like it because it makes me think about how it looks. It paints a picture in my mind."

Beakish nose. "I like it because it's funny. She is not a very nice person and this makes her sound like a bird."

Her icy voice droned on. "I like it because it's creepy. It adds on to what we know about her. She is a horrible person to Norah and Gavin."

She felt as slack as a rag doll. "I like it because you can picture what she's feeling."

Filled with Christmas pudding, cakes, tins of fruit and fish. "I like it because it makes me feel hungry."

The brightest and the plumpest. "It reminds me of Christmas."

Rippling lake. "It sounds peaceful."

Later in the novel (pages 78–102), when Norah and Gavin are settled at Aunt Flo's house in Toronto and Norah is starting school, Alexa was a discussion director, asking questions and making predictions: "I think Norah will have lots of friends at school. What will happen if she doesn't? Aunt Florence seems really strict. She might send Norah to go to other people. Gavin seems spoiled. I wonder if Norah gets mad. She probably will."

The Role of the Teacher in Class Novel Study

During discussions, we move from group to group, evaluating whether or not the work has been done by placing a check mark in a record book. We listen to the discussions but try not to direct the conversations. Like a sports coach, we can advise but we cannot play the game. We act as mediator for the large-group discussions and we model process. We try to extend the thinking by asking open-ended questions and questions that clarify the students' comments. We model ways of talking. Following are some specific guidelines.

Ways to facilitate discussion

Encourage students to provide more detail:

"Can you tell me more about that idea?"

"What makes you think that?"

Clarify and extend meaning:

"Say more about that."

"Can you explain that, please?"

"Could it be...?"

"Do you mean...?"

Promote inferential and critical thinking:

"Why do you think that?"

"What's your evidence?"

"Where in the text did you see that?"

Encourage polite interactions:

"Thank you."

"I am not disagreeing with you, but..."

"Do you have anything more to add?"

"Let's look at the other side of this."

Finally, we want to know what overall impressions the students have taken from the book. Have they found the main ideas? Do they understand the dilemmas faced by the various characters and see how they were motivated to behave the way they did? Could they synthesize the novel effectively? Jan set a final assignment to be completed by everyone. In the role of one of the characters, the students wrote at least three diary entries from three different moments in the story. The diaries of the characters revealed that the students had indeed taken a great deal of understanding from the book, as this short sample from Katrina's writing shows.

Diary of Norah

Thursday August 15th, 1940:

Today I fed the chickens and went to help the Sky Watchers. Just after dinner

Mum and Dad asked to see me privately in my room. Oh no! I thought. Could they possibly want me to go to Canada? Tom said I would be a coward if I went to Canada. But it's true. They want me and Gavin to leave on the next voyage to Canada. Granddad came into the room halfway through our talking. He said that he had nothing to do with it. I'm trying hard not to look scared. But deep down I'm very scared. Who am I going to live with?

—Norah Stokes, age 10

What Next?

In the next phase, small groups form and read a book together, with each role being represented each time in the group. Several sets of four books at a variety of reading levels are needed. We give book talks to promote interest in each of the books and have children sign up for the book they want to read. To make it easier to form the groups, we often have children write down their top three choices. Once groups are formed, they each divide their novel into eight chunks to be read in preparation for two discussion groups per week. They assign each group member a role for each chunk of the story, rotating so that everyone plays each role twice. Schedules are set up with the groups so they know exactly how much to read for each due date. Tell them that keeping up-to-date is of vital importance; this is work that cannot be missed, as it lets down the rest of the group when one person has not done his part. As Samantha said in the interviews: "Also, it's kind of a commitment because you have to remember to do your part, or your group is going to suffer."

What About Vocabulary Development and Collecting the Gifts of Words?

Did literature circles help develop word consciousness? We feel that they were pivotal in moving students toward independence as word-conscious learners. The word hunter role proved to be the most popular of all the roles. Students love to pounce on simile, metaphor, and alliteration as obvious Gifts of Words. They moan if an author doesn't (apparently) use any Gifts of Words. Here is the start of sensitivity toward language in general. We saw growing awareness of how authors use language to make a point. Not all rich language is necessarily so obvious, and not all writing needs to be flowery to be powerful. What makes for strong writing? Can we see why a writer chose to use a particular style, a turn of phrase, or a particular word?

The reasons given for the choice of Gifts of Words range from the personal ("Because it reminds me of Christmas") to the sensory ("Because I can almost smell it"). Often, students simply say, "Because it is very descriptive" or "It makes a strong picture in my mind." While this is rudimentary, it shows that the student has understood the role of language in communicating accurately and powerfully with the reader. Language in literature is not an add-on or fringe benefit: it is part of the overall form and feeling of the work of art. Words, their meanings, syntax, sounds, rhythms, and images all contribute to the complete sensation of the writing. The effect on the reader depends upon the reader's sensitivity to the nuances and subtleties of the language. If we can begin the process of sensitizing young readers to language in the elementary and middle school years, we can help them improve not only as readers but also as writers.

During each novel series, we have each novel-study group compile a list of their favorite Gifts of Words on chart paper. The charts are displayed for the whole class to ponder, and the class votes on the Gifts of Words that warrant being added to the bank. Individuals are encouraged to collect their personal favorites, record them in their wordcatchers or on small strips, and store them in their writer's toolkit, which will be introduced in the next chapter.

Out of the Mouths of Learners: Observations From the Students

When asked, "Has doing this group work made you a better reader?" one group of students replied as follows:

GABRIELLA: Yes, because you have to look carefully for different words.

ALISON: Yes, because most of the time you just read through the book and go, "Oh, that's nice," then pick another book, but now, you talk about it and pick out different things.

KAITLIN: And if you don't understand something, you can ask your group and they can tell you what it means or you can take their guess.

ALISON: Yes, 'cause now you're more on the lookout for things and you think about them more. You become more aware of things.

GABRIELLA: You sort of compare books. You become so aware that each book is different, say, that book had the most questions but this book had more Gifts of Words.

AMANDA: So you're more aware. One book has this, and one book has that. You see them on the library shelf and you think they look the same but they're not. They're, like, totally different.

KAITLIN: It gives you ideas when you write your own stories if you're a word hunter.

AMANDA: Yes, you can use the Gifts of Words in your own writing.

YUKIO: You find a neat word and you list it in your book and say why it's neat.

BRETT: It gives you a good picture of what's actually happening.

Thoughts to Ponder

As the vocabulary group met over the course of several years, discussion about literature circles was a central theme. What are some of the things we learned?

- All of us saw animated conversations take place.

- We saw the eager way in which the groups got down to work. Each group adopted territory of its own in the classroom and got settled right away, plopping down on the cushions or drawing their chairs toward the tables to get closer to each other. They clearly enjoyed the process and felt comfortable with it.

- We saw less able readers shine in discussion. In several cases it was necessary for those students to receive help with the reading, as their own reading ability was at a lower level than that required by the book their group had chosen. However, "talking" books, and parents or siblings who read aloud those chapters that would be discussed at school, helped those students over this hurdle.

- All of us found that we had groups that needed slightly easier books to read. And we also had other groups that raced through titles and needed to be challenged.

- Some titles were not enjoyed as much as others, but the small-group dynamics kept the students reading to the end, when they might have abandoned the book if they had been reading on their own.

- Most students from grade 5 onward showed themselves to be capable of sustaining on-task discussion for at least ten minutes. The majority of groups worked for 15 to 20 minutes. Some groups regularly continued for the full 40 minutes. On occasion, an audiotape recorder was placed at one of the tables, and the students knew that their conversation would be heard later by the teacher. This provided an extra incentive for concentration on the topic at hand!

- The journals were key to the success of the group discussions. If students had not written in their journals, it was harder for them to participate in the talk. The role of journal writing was to provide a scaffold for the talk. As the groups became more skilled, the journal writing was used as a jumping-off point for discussion rather than providing the sole content. The writing forced the students to think ahead so that, in the group work, they were ready with something to say. We saw the language of book talk developing and students engaged with the literature in very meaningful ways, behaving like real readers (Scott & Wells, 1998).

- As students talked, they actually listened to each other, and taking turns with the journals proved to be a significant feature of the process. They nodded in agreement as points were made, or interrupted to question if someone made a statement with which they disagreed. They opened their books and found support for their ideas or clarified misunderstandings. The children genuinely knew what happened in the story and developed insights into plot structure, character motivation, and the values issues that arise in all good literature.

- Once the culture and environment of the reading program were established and the social aspect was developed, our students never wanted to read individually without talking to anyone! The talking and sharing of ideas became the focal point of the whole program. This is what we had hoped for—students using their writing as a prop for meaningful dialogue. Of course, this culture does not exist everywhere, and our hope is that these students will take these ways of thinking into their future classrooms, and that they will become more thoughtful readers, having internalized different ways of interacting with a text. Yet, just as important, we hope this kind of talk will transfer when they ponder the dilemmas of writing their own stories.

—— ✳ ——

Chapter 6

Writing Together

Scaffolding Writing Through Whole-Class Activities

I need to check my work properly; check for punctuation, check C.A.R.E.S.,
see if I need any Gift of Words, just don't rush through it.
—Gurpreet, grade 6

In this chapter, we describe how to use the Bank of Powerful Language in whole-class writing activities. Through this type of scaffolding, we give students tools of the trade with which they can craft their writing. We show students how to withdraw words from the bank to make their pieces sound more like the books they read.

As your Bank of Powerful Language grows, it should contain many strong words, phrases, or sentences found in read-alouds and independent reading. We've discussed how these words and phrases are deposited in the bank in previous chapters. This chapter builds on the bank with specific writing skills and scaffolded instruction in writing.

Tools of the Trade

Once students have entered into the culture of reading and writing in our classrooms and are beginning to write with confidence, there are many skills that need to be taught. We want students to experiment and play with language, to develop their own voice and style, to be excited and capable writers. This does not happen through osmosis, with our merely telling them to apply more effort. It comes through direct teaching of the skills that writers need. Students want to improve, but too often we have let them develop naturally. Therefore, we have taken a cue from Lucy Calkins and her chapter titled, "Don't Be Afraid to Teach: Tools to Help Us Create Mini-Lessons" (Calkins, 1994). Every profession needs a toolbox. Mechanics have a toolbox with wrenches, oil, and a grease gun; builders have screwdrivers, saws, hammers, and nails; doctors have medical bags with a stethoscope, bandages, and pills; painters have easels, paints, and brushes. What does a writer need in his or her "toolbox"?

We think that students need tools to help them think about alternative words, tools to help them remember the conventions of English, tools to remind them to pay attention to elements of style, and whatever tools we can create to help them enrich the power of their writing.

WRITER'S TOOLKIT

What good are these "tools" if they cannot be found or immediately implemented to create meaningful writing? One solution is to introduce the writer's toolkit. These are pizza boxes donated from a local store, filled with the contents from mini-lessons and anchor lessons like the ones in this chapter. Each student's box holds all her tools, including her writer's notebook. In Bonnie's class, the writer's toolkit contained a core spelling list, a wordcatcher, lesson cards, "rules for" cards, personal favorite Gifts of Words strips, steps in the writing process cards, and a proofreading checklist. This is the place to include any lesson or tip you think your students could use as writers.

Writing the lessons, rules, and checklists on card stock (often available as discards from printing companies) works well to keep the tools from turning into crumbled wads of paper. They also last long enough for students to carry forward as a toolkit (if needed) when they leave your room.

Wordcatchers

The Bank of Powerful Language can take many forms. In Chapter 2, we discussed the use of a bulletin board for collecting words, and in Chapter 3, we described a Shades of Meaning tree. A third form for collecting powerful words and phrases can be individual collections in booklets called wordcatchers.

These booklets can either be shaped like a baseball glove by cutting paper to follow the design in Figure 6-1, or created on regular paper with the glove in the middle (Figure 6-2). You can supply some of the words to get students started, or students can collect the words entirely on their

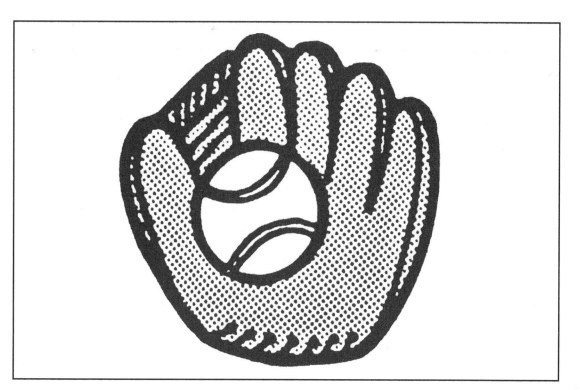

Fig. 6-1: Wordcatcher Booklet Cover

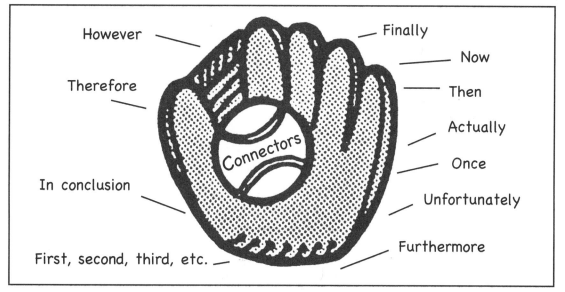

Fig. 6-2: The Wordcatcher in Play

own. The pages in the wordcatcher can have different categories, such as connecting words, color words, vivid verbs, and ideal idioms, or contain shades of meaning for commonly used words such as *said*, *big*, *small*, and *scare*. The organization is up to you and your students, and we encourage you to try out different options. These booklets provide readily accessible alternatives for widely used words and offer students a space to write their favorite Gifts of Words. These repositories of powerful language are useful tools that can be used in students' writing throughout the year.

MAKING SURE WITH MINI-LESSONS

Some "tools" are the topics we teach in mini-lessons or through whole-class writing assignments. These tools, or skills, cover a range of craft elements that writers need, from the gathering of ideas through crafting sentences, word choice, organization of paragraphs, leads, conclusions, and the conventions of language.

As the year progresses, we keep a list of the mini-lessons we have taught and post it on the classroom wall. Students refer to these tools as they write. Here are examples of the things we teach in mini-lessons:

- Finding fresh ideas
- Using punctuation marks
- Using dialogue
- Avoiding run-on sentences
- Crafting figurative language, free of clichés
- Showing rather than telling
- Describing characters
- Finding exciting leads
- Bringing text to its conclusion
- Using powerful language

These are not only the tools needed during the revision and proofreading steps of the writing process but the strategies writers rely on time and time again. They include techniques for helping writers clarify their meanings, organize their writing, add voice, and use powerful language. We call this part of our program "making sure." Students have a notebook, file folder, or pizza box where they store their tools. When we notice a particular issue or writing problem, we develop a mini-lesson. Students use their notebooks to reflect on the lesson and record key ideas.

A good question to ask them to write about in their notebook is, How will you use what you have learned in this mini-lesson in your next piece of writing? Mini-lessons can be directed formally to the whole class or can be impromptu, during conferences with individual students. Mini-lessons are what the name implies—short and tightly constrained (Atwell, 1987; Calkins, 1994). However, depending on the topic and the involvement of students, mini-lessons sometimes turn into discussions and cover a range of concerns.

We search for anything that will help our students learn writing skills. We do not teach these from a single resource book or sequentially page by page. Rather, we teach them as we see the problem arise in students' writing from observing or conferencing. Rubrics and rating scales also help us to decide what we want to teach. Assessment provides a springboard for the design of mini-lessons, and for conversations with students. As Ruth Culham noted in *6+1 Traits of Writing* (2003), "Assessment only provides an indication of where a piece of writing is at any given moment. It's not a final evaluation of the student as writer. We use the assessment to foster the conversation between writer and reader" (p. 14). Rubrics for the assessment of student writing are to be found in Chapters 7–11.

As we teach these lessons, we try to use trade books as our texts. Remember, modeling is an important aspect of learning. Seeing how other authors use the skills creates both a model for imitation and an awareness of why these skills might be useful. Also, by using models, we are likely to elicit patterns and ideas from student observations instead of telling them about the skill. This is a much more effective and engaging way to communicate information. Students are the ones doing the thinking and making the connections instead of hearing predigested material that may flow in one ear and out the other. The work of writers for children is an amazing resource for teachers. It provides a hook with which we catch the enthusiasm of our students.

ANCHOR LESSONS

When we really want to anchor the topic of a mini-lesson in memory and in students' craft as writers, it takes more than a few minutes, and the students need to practice the skill by writing a piece that incorporates the new learning. We call these lessons "anchor lessons" (Wells & Reid, 2004). The following examples of lessons we taught all build a valuable bank of experience that students can draw upon in their independent writing. Writing as a class, sharing each other's efforts to write on a particular topic, and developing the criteria that define an excellent piece of writing—these lessons build confidence and stamina. They are the scaffolds that support our student writers as they develop and grow. We add the names of the anchor lessons to the growing list of mini-lessons and refer the students to it often. "Do you remember when we did the anchor lesson about Very Important People? You learned how to ask fat questions. I want to hear fat questions being asked."

Create a Very Important People Book

Here is one specific activity that we found useful for finding out about each other and gaining knowledge about writing. One of the most important things we develop in the first weeks of school is the culture of our classroom. Building community by recognizing the individual talents of our students and connecting with one another are central goals as we frame the year to come. Reading aloud and sharing in a literature circle are two ways in which we consciously work toward these goals.

In the first weeks of school, students interview each other, asking interesting and intriguing questions. Student are taught about different questioning techniques, which are outlined on a poster describing fat and skinny questions (Bellanca & Fogarty, 1991)

Fat Questions	Skinny Questions
Fat questions require lots of discussion and explanation with interesting examples. Fat questions take time to think through and answer in depth. Fat questions begin with *how*, *why*, or *what if*.	Skinny questions require simple yes/no/maybe or one-word answers or a nod or shake of the head. They take up no space. Skinny questions begin with *what*, *where*, and *when*.

While the students write and publish copies of their interviews, we take a photograph of each student. Then each interview and photograph is decorated and mounted. All pages are assembled and coil-bound into a book titled "Very Important People in [the name of the class]." The book is displayed on an easel by the door for all visitors and parents to see. Every night a different student takes the book home so his or her parents can "meet" the class. When new students enter the class, we assign someone to interview them and add a page to the book.

This acknowledgment of the individuals who make up the class, the cultural capital that they bring in the door, and the connections to their lives outside of school help establish the idea that we care about our students as people. This idea goes a long way in helping them feel connected to our school and our class.

Create Great Titles

One of the first writing lessons we developed came out of the labels that we saw our students using as titles for their stories, such as "My Vacation," "My Dog," and "A Funny Time." We decided to try to change that pattern by looking at the titles used in real books. Students went to the library to find five books with titles they liked. We discussed why the titles caught their attention and compiled what we had learned onto a chart that stayed visible in the room and was added to each student's toolkit for later reference.

Great Titles

- Say something about the story
- Often highlight the main idea, theme, or event
- State where the story takes place
- Can ask a question
- Name the main character

Create Great Leads

The same technique can be used to look at effective ways authors begin their stories. We begin by reading the opening paragraphs of four different books, choosing books that begin differently, such as these popular choices:

- *Who Is Francis Rain?* by Margaret Buffie begins with the author talking directly to the reader: *To be fair, I'd better warn you. If you don't believe in ghosts, and if you doubt that you could ever be convinced that they exist, it might be best to stop reading right about here.*

- *Hero of Lesser Causes* by Julie Johnston begins by hinting at what is going to happen: *It started off as a peaceful, plodding kind of summer, the summer of 1946. We didn't know that our lives would charge wildly out of control.*

- *Sour Land* by William H. Armstrong begins with dialogue, introduces characters, and highlights a main issue in the story: *"Why is one kind of graveyard called a cemetery and the other a burying ground?" David Stone asked his father as they paused at a point where a high wire fence ran at right angles down the hill from Anson Stone's pasture fence.*

  "They bury Negroes in one and us in the other." Jonathan Stone interrupted before his father could answer.

- *Because of Winn-Dixie* by Kate DiCamillo opens with first-person narrative and establishes the voice of the main character: *My name is India Opal Buloni, and last summer my daddy, the preacher, sent me to the store for a box of macaroni-and-cheese, some white rice, and two tomatoes and I came back with a dog.*

Discussing these leads with students helps them identify how authors begin books. Next, we send them to the classroom or school library to find out how other books might start. When they bring back various examples, we discuss what the author is trying to do with each lead and record the different types of leads on chart paper.

Kinds of Leads
- Dialogue—characters talking to each other
- Author talking to the reader
- Description of setting (where the story takes place)
- Description of what happened, followed by the story of how it happened
- Action right away
- Questions characters ask of themselves or of the reader
- Introduction of a mystery or issue
- Character talking to himself or herself
- Author giving hints about what might happen

In order for students to internalize the type of writing we want to see, they must have the opportunity to practice new strategies. A familiar story, such as *Little Red Riding Hood*, provides the opportunity to concentrate on their skill of writing a good lead. We divide the class into five or six groups, asking each group to write a different kind of lead for *Little Red Riding Hood* from the chart. Groups then present their leads to the full class. The final step is to display this chart in the classroom and add it to the toolkit to be used for the rest of the year.

Create Active Dialogue

Once a large number of students start writing dialogue, it is time to look at possible alternatives to the word *said*. This is a natural lead-in to the Shades of Meaning tree discussed in Chapter 3. We scour books to find different verbs used for talking, discuss the shades of meaning, and add them to the tree, the Bank of Powerful Language, and/or the student wordcatchers.

In Other Words: Alternatives to *Said*

exclaimed	*whispered*	*groaned*	*shouted*	*snarled*
yelled	*replied*	*snapped*	*hissed*	*muttered*

This list grows as time goes on, with students discovering ever more creative ways to say *said*.

SCAFFOLDING WRITING WITH CUE CARDS

The purpose of anchor lessons is to help students remember and use the skills that are being taught. However, we found that the creation and use of cue cards along with the lessons facilitated their understanding and helped them become aware of craft elements of writing as well as sources of confusion. These cards were usually developed on 8½" x 11" card stock or smaller, with magnetic strips attached to the back. The magnets allowed them to be easily mounted on the whiteboard and easily removed to desks to aid individual writers.

Show Don't Tell Cards

This tool was developed because, although we had done an exercise on the differences between telling something (e.g., I was mad) and showing what that looked or felt like, we did not see the hoped-for change in students' writing. Through discussion with other teachers, we decided the problem was not that students didn't understand the concept; they just needed further scaffolding. Students needed lots of writing samples, ready and available to borrow, with well-constructed "showing" sentences. Hence, the Show Don't Tell cards came into being as models.

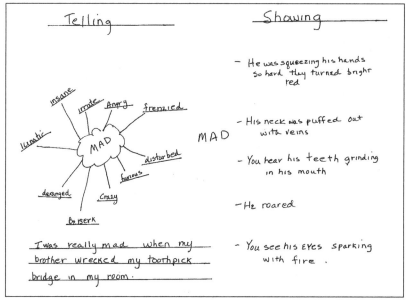

Fig. 6-3: Show Don't Tell Card

In this activity, students, in groups, brainstorm ideas and find sentences in their notebooks that state a feeling such as *I was ignored* or *I was mad*. These "telling" sentences are written on the board and students choose a sentence that they think they and their group will use in their writing. This is a key point, because this exercise could amount to a cutesy activity. The whole intent here is to produce an aid to scaffold students' writing. The sentences have to be usable, something that students will borrow. Once the decision is made, they begin to draft "showing" sentences that are revised by both their group and the teacher. Once they are happy with their work, they produce a card (see Figure 6-3). On one half of a card the group writes its "telling" sentence—*John was happy*, for example. Below, the word *happy* is circled and as many synonyms as possible are webbed. On the second half of the card, three or more "showing" sentences are recorded—for example, *John leaped in the air, hugged his best friend, and yelled, "YES!" when he saw his report card.*

Simile Cards

In developing word consciousness, the important point is to encourage students to examine and experiment with forms of language that they may not realize exist. Focusing students' attention on figurative language is an extremely powerful tool for teaching students to improve their writing. Their first collected Gifts of Words are, more often than not, similes. Similes are far easier to understand and to personalize than are metaphors or idioms.

Once our students discovered that using similes was a way to improve their writing, we started seeing similes in every piece of work. To avoid cliché-driven writing, we developed simile cards. In this activity, students discuss clichés and why they should be avoided.

The following poem by Eve Merriam (1986) is a wonderful way to introduce clichés and their alternatives.

Cliché
by Eve Merriam

… A cliché is
what we all say
when we're too lazy
to find another way
and so we say

warm as toast

quiet as a mouse

slow as molasses

quick as a wink

Think

Is toast the warmest thing you know?

Think again, it might be so.

Think again: it might even be snow!

Soft as lamb's wool, fleecy snow,

a lacy shawl of new-fallen snow.

Listen to that mouse go

scuttling and clawing,

nibbling and pawing.

A mouse can speak

if only a squeak.

Is a mouse the quietest thing you know?

Think again, it might not be so.

Think again: it might be a shadow.

Quiet as a shadow,

quiet as growing grass,

quiet as a pillow,

or a looking glass.

Slow as molasses,

quick as a wink.

Before you say so,

take time to think.

Slow as time passes

when you're sad and alone;

quick as an hour can go

happily on your own.

After discussing this poem, generate a number of class examples of similes that work well.
Then, individually or in small groups, have students choose a simile to develop as an illustrated

example (see Figure 6-4). When the simile cards are complete, laminate them and add them to the class Bank of Powerful Language.

While some of the simile cards work better than others, the point is to help all students think about and develop ways to express their ideas using more powerful language. Sometimes students developed wonderful examples; others didn't quite work!

> As hot as a desert, he stormed out of the room in a frenzy. (Harman, grade 6)

> As big as an elephant steamrolling over his domain of tundra. (Ian, grade 6)

Please recognize that these first attempts are their approximations in developing the discourse of published authors and that good writing develops with time and feedback. The important point is that they are experimenting with word choice and language use within a framework that can give them constructive feedback.

Fig. 6-4: Simile Card

Idiom Cards

Idioms are a particularly difficult form of language for English learners. In previous years, we had tried to teach idioms using a worksheet matching idioms with their meanings. Most of the idioms were unfamiliar to our students and completing the worksheet was torturous for everyone. We had to explain what each idiom meant and, often, how the idiom originated in order for them to succeed at this task. An "aha" moment came when we realized that most languages have idioms, although they differ from language to language. So now we enlist parental help in explaining and discussing idioms of our students' native languages. This way, students can develop the concept of what idioms are and realize that such phrases as *it's raining cats and dogs* are not to be taken literally.

Then we provide a list of English idioms and engage in a whole-class discussion about their possible meanings. Each students selects one idiom with the task of illustrating the literal meaning, writing what the idiom means, and giving an example by using it in a sentence. Our students have great fun with this activity. (See a sample card in Figure 6-5.) When the cards are completed, students guess each other's idioms, given the picture of the literal meaning. Of course, the completed idiom cards are added to the bank.

BACK COVER: Idiom: *It's raining cats and dogs.*	FRONT COVER: 
INSIDE RIGHT: Definition: *It's raining very heavily.*	INSIDE LEFT: Use in context: *I'm soaked! It's raining cats and dogs outside.*

Fig. 6-5: Idiom Card

Homonym Cards

Tracking homonym errors in our students' writing can help us target instruction on persistent errors. Similar to the way they created the idiom cards, students were asked to illustrate the various meanings of words such as *pair*, *pare*, and *pear*. (See Figure 6-6.) Again, these were added to our bank.

Fig. 6-6: Homonym Card

Scaffolding Writing Through Whole-Class Activities

As the toolkit is being developed, it is important to provide multiple and various opportunities to practice using powerful language. Writing in short segments to emphasize word choice and creating class books offer students occasions to apply what they are learning with strong support.

USING DRAMA TO CREATE WORD AWARENESS

Our colleague Teresa Blackstone developed several drama activities and shared them with our group. Drama in the classroom can bring events, emotions, and experiences to life. Abstract ideas become more concrete; thoughts, feelings and sensations are brought to the surface, and words to express these are generated. There are many drama activities that can be a precursor to writing, helping the students to imagine scenarios and developing vocabulary that can be used to enrich the writing. For instance, shades of meaning for *walk* can be put on cards and drawn randomly from a basket; then students try to guess the verb for the pantomimed action. Students can also act out short scenarios while class members record their actions in words. Students soon learn to tiptoe, or slither, or bound onto the "scene," and the students watching learn to match their words with the actions. As a result, students become more observant of nonverbal communication as well as the actor's tone of voice.

Drama reinforces the idea that writers show what happens using descriptive language rather than simply telling about it. ("His knees crumpled and he fell to the ground" as opposed to "He was exhausted.") It is a fun way to learn and practice words, reinforce meaning, enhance word awareness, increase motivation, and develop social skills such as cooperation with others. It also provides a concrete, visual tool for revision of students' writing. When another person acts out their words, students can see whether the words captured the action they meant to convey.

Practicing New Words by Acting Them Out

In this activity, groups of two or three students choose words or phrases from the Bank of Powerful Language, or you may choose a target word you wish them to learn. They ensure that they understand the definitions of the words by discussing among themselves the precise meaning and checking in the dictionary if necessary. For example:

Officer Delinko let out an involuntary whimper. (Hiaasen, *Hoot*, p. 43)

Next, they write their own sentence using the target word.

John let out an involuntary cry of pain when he broke his ankle.

The sentence is then developed into a short descriptive paragraph that the students act out in front of the rest of the class. (Restrict the scene to one location, and one moment in time. This is not about writing a whole story with many episodes.) The paragraphs are then exchanged among the groups and students act out each other's scenes, thus experiencing all the target words. This procedure can be followed and repeated several times during the reading of a class novel.

Retelling a Story by Developing Sensory Language

Share with students a picture book that has action and a simple story line. Folktales work well, as do fractured fairy tales such as *The Three Little Wolves and the Big Bad Pig* by Eugene Trivizas.

Divide the class into groups and assign a section of the story to each group for retelling. Each group has a narrator and the students act out the parts, exaggerating the actions. Following each scene, the class brainstorms words to describe the characters' actions and emotions. The actors describe how they felt at various times during the skit. Record these words on charts or on the blackboard.

Students then rewrite their section of the story, using as much descriptive language as possible. They refer to the charts and to their own experience as a character in the story. The finished products can be combined into class books.

Exploring a Moment in Time: Dramatizing Specific Scenarios

Student writing can be much improved if specific moments are stretched to include details: the moment when a winning lottery ticket was opened; the time when the Ferris wheel broke down, leaving riders stranded at the top; the moment when a beloved pet was taken to the vet to be put to sleep; the time a swimmer in the ocean felt a slippery shape brush past her body. Short scenarios such as these provide a starting point for the drama.

Groups of two or three students receive teacher-generated scenarios on cards. Their job is to act out the scene, pretending to be the characters and showing their feelings through actions and words. They are to focus on emotions and show rather than tell how the characters react.

Some prompts to encourage the action are:

> What did you feel when…?
> How did your body react when…?
> What did you say?
> What else did you do?

The groups perform their scenes and create a final tableau, or frozen moment, in which the emotions are exaggerated. The class lists the words they see demonstrated (*fear*, *terror*, *apprehension*, *nervousness*, etc.). They describe what they see their classmates doing.

Students then complete the scenario by writing the rest of the story using descriptive language and stretching the moment to provide details of the emotions. Here are five sample scenarios.

Scenario 1

It was a glorious sunny day when we went swimming off the reef. I adjusted my face mask and dove down to see the colorful tropical fish. My friend was nearby and she gave me a cheerful wave before diving deeper to explore behind a rock. Suddenly, a large, slimy shape brushed past my body and…

Scenario 2

We were camping in the mountains. My parents were asleep in their tent and I was snuggled in my warm sleeping bag. Suddenly a piercing scream shattered the silence. I…

Scenario 3

I had trained for weeks for the big race. I was jogging five miles a day and eating really healthy food. My chances of becoming school record holder were good and I was very excited. On the morning of sports day, I woke up feeling sick. My stomach ached and my head was spinning. "You'll have to stay home today," said Mom. I…

Scenario 4

My beautiful cat, Angel, is 19 years old. She has become very weak and feeble. Her back legs are dragging and we are taking her to the vet today. "It is kinder to put her to sleep," says Mom. I carry her to her traveling basket and put her inside. We drive downtown to the vet's office. As we go inside…

Scenario 5

We were visiting the city for the first time. We live in the country, so it was very exciting to be downtown among skyscrapers and the busy traffic. It seemed so new and strange. We all went down into the subway, and trains were rushing past with gusts of hot air. I got on the train and looked around for my parents. They were nowhere to be seen…

USING CHERISHED BOOKS AS MODELS FOR WRITING CLASS BOOKS

After our students were inundated with powerful language, we leaned toward letting them loose to write. However, we found that this is when explicit scaffolding in the form of class books is particularly effective. They need to hear, see, and experiment with uncomplicated texts. Cherished picture books and poems serve this purpose. They can provide models for developing a class book. A class book allows each student to perform within his or her own zone of proximal development, to produce only one or two pages, and to author an impressive product. Like reading aloud and shared reading, creating a class book is a more highly scaffolded activity than independent writing. Through this process, elements of style can be addressed more completely, and a model for individual books is created.

In interviews, students identified writing class books as one of the most influential exercises in our program. They enjoyed the process of working together, and during the school year, these demonstrations and models improved the quality of student published pages.

Finding and Using a Cherished Book

A cherished book contains a compelling pattern or simple plotline that can be imitated to provide support for a class writing project. The formats that writers use can also be borrowed as wonderful hooks upon which we can hang our original ideas. Pointing out these frames and patterns can enlighten novice writers. When we read *The Pain and the Great One* (Blume, 1974), for example, we hear two alternating voices. What a great idea for telling a story! In *The Jolly Postman* (Ahlberg, 2001), characters send letters to each other, creating another interesting way to engage the reader in the story. Many books have cumulative patterns and refrains that work well in starting class writing projects. Different books provide different models for writing, and it is important to choose books that meet your purpose. A list of books that we've found useful for particular models is shown in the box on page 106.

The steps to using a cherished book are fairly straightforward:

1. Introduce a cherished book by reading it aloud to the class.
2. Discuss and examine how the book can be used to scaffold student writing.
3. In groups, generate ideas for pages and discuss appropriate, effective language.
4. Publish as a class or group project.

This last step can be left as a choice for individual writing projects.

Following are examples of how we use picture books to develop collaborative class books that focus on word consciousness. Many other books will work if the teacher is passionate about the story, the illustrations, or the format. Find a book that will scaffold student writing and have fun with it!

Animalia by Graeme Base

This alphabet book focuses on language, word choice, and expanding vocabulary knowledge. Base uses alliteration to create a sentence for each letter of the alphabet. In addition, each page is filled with illustrations of other words that start with the same letter. For instance, the letter *L* has *Lazy lions lounging in the local library* with lizards, lilies, lobsters, lichen, and llamas in the background.

After a writing lesson on alliteration, students read the book, look for Base (who is hidden in each picture), and try to identify all the illustrated words for each letter. Identifying these pictures often extends the vocabulary of students in the class.

To create a community book, each student or group chooses a letter and creates a page modeled on *Animalia*. All pages are collected and bound into one volume. Students illustrated these sentences, adding numerous letter-related images (e.g., mushrooms, mountains, mice):

Macho monkeys mingling merrily at the mall.
Hundreds of harried horses head home to hide.
Plump pirate penguins poke piñatas.

Q is for Duck by Mary Elting and Michael Folsom

This alphabet book is written as a guessing game. Each page asks a question and the reader must flip the page to get the answer. On the first page, the author asks, "Q is for Duck. Why?" On the next page, she states, "Because a duck quacks."

Some of Our Favorite Cherished Picture Books

Ahlberg, Janet and Allan, *The Jolly Postman*
Angelou, Maya, *Life Doesn't Frighten Me*
Base, Graeme, *Animalia*
Baylor, Byrd, *Everybody Needs a Rock*
Bouchard, Dave, *If You're Not From the Prairie*
Brown, Margaret Wise, *The Important Book*
Browne, Anthony, *My Dad*
Elting, Mary, and Folsom, Michael, *Q is for Duck*
Hundal, Nancy, *I Heard My Mother Call My Name*
Laden, Nina, *The Night I Followed the Dog*
Scieszka, Jon, and Smith, Lane, *The True Story of the Three Little Pigs*

Fig. 6-7: Using *Q Is for Duck* as a Model for Writing

After reading this book and discussing the pattern, students began to expand the one-word answer modeled in the text by adding more descriptive words and phrases. One alphabet letter is given to each student, who produces both the question and answer for the class version of the book (see Figure 6-7). Here are some samples written by students:

E is for Apple. Why? Because you enormously enjoy eating it.

F is for Elephant. Why? Because an elephant has folds and folds of fat and is fabulous to ride.

P is for Castle. Why? Because some people picture it as a princely palace where a proud princess parades in peace.

S is for Night. Why? Because the night is seriously silent.

Each page is illustrated, mounted on tagboard, and then coil-bound into a class book that is added to the class library. Using their previous knowledge of alliteration, students enjoy this delightful and easy activity that requires them to play with language.

***The Important Book* by Margaret Wise Brown**

This patterned book of descriptive phrases can be used for any content. It starts and ends with the same phrase, with a series of descriptive sentences in between. Read aloud the book to students and ask them to discuss the pattern. Once the pattern has been discovered, the class brainstorms a variety of nouns and identifies their important attributes. Writing groups are then established, and each group chooses two nouns from the list. Each group develops its own versions of the two pages on chart paper, modeled after *The Important Book*.

When all the groups have completed their pages, their first drafts are placed around the room. The groups travel around the room, reading other groups' work. They write suggestions for additions or substitutions, focusing on improving word choice. The authors return to their own writing to make final decisions about their piece and produce a publishable page. The pages and illustrations are then bound together and published in a class book.

An extension activity has students creating their own individual versions of *The Important Book*. Each student chooses eight important things, with the last page being about themselves. For example: "The important thing about me is that I am me." Following are two examples by sixth graders.

The important thing about the Moon
is that it is the light that leads us
into night.
It guards the sky and bounces off stars.
It is the father of all of your dreams.
It laughs at you when you have
to go to bed.
But the most important thing about the Moon
is that it is the light that leads
us into night.
—Janet, grade 6

The important thing about Laughter
is that if you don't let it out
you will explode!
It is a jumble hitting the sides
of your stomach

trying to get out!

It is an international link

everybody does it!

But the most important thing about Laughter

is that if you don't let it out,

you will explode!

—Arlo, grade 6

I Heard My Mother Call My Name by **Nancy Hundal**

This book reminds us of when we were children and made up excuses to stay outside and play longer. Every kid can identify with this story and the language is beautiful.

Begin by asking students to list all the things they do outside after dinner and to circle their favorites. Next, have them convert their favorites into an excuse they can use with their parents that they then share with the class. After reading the book again, discuss the pattern, the language, and the excuses. Their assignment is to produce a double page with the writing on the left-hand page and an illustration on the right-hand page. Their excuse has to incorporate powerful language and can be from their list, ideas from the book, or a similar idea. Each page ends with "I heard my mother call my name. I know I should go in . . ." (Turn the page and find the excuse.)

I heard my mother call my name. I know I should go in . . .

But a ton of monstrous disgusting creatures chased me far from home. When the sun crashed from the sky, the creatures, who were petrified of the dark, slipped away through the shadows of the night. (Rory, grade 6)

I heard my mother call my name. I know I should go in . . .

But I saw the shadows of two dogs dancing down the street. I looked back but there was nothing there. Curious, I wanted to know what was going on, so I tipped-toed down the street. (Katrina, grade 6)

STUDENT VOICES

"Komal, Raman and I work really well together. My best story this year was the picture book we wrote together." —Jesse, grade 6

Making Use of the Writer's Toolkit

Class projects such as these give us opportunities to reinforce the use of the items in the writer's toolkits. We check to see that students are indeed opening their pizza boxes and using the resources inside. Are they using their wordcatchers? Are they looking at the rubrics and rating scales we provide, to help them focus on what they need to do? Here are a few more tools we have found helpful.

ReVISION

Once students draft a piece of writing that they plan to publish, they must work with the piece to make it shine. We call this ReVision and purposely spell it as one word with a capital V. This word means to "look again" or to "see with new eyes." Students become editors who take a fresh look at their writing and apply the ReVision skills of combining, adding, rearranging, eliminating, and substituting. It is through this process that teachers can help students learn how to improve and to refine their pieces. Once ReVision is complete, the piece of writing is "set" and ready to be proofread.

The following acronym was developed by Julie Corday, a teacher from Delta School District in British Columbia, Canada.

An *Editor* Is Someone Who C.A.R.E.S.

Combines sentences that are too short and choppy

Adds more information or details

Rearranges words or sentences to make them sound better

Eliminates any unnecessary words, information, or sentences

Substitutes more powerful language for telling or weak language

Each student is given a copy of these guidelines mounted on colored tagboard to keep in her toolkit.

PROOFREADING

Through this step, the students correct the mechanics of their pieces. We use the analogy of taking a car to the garage for a tune-up. Unlike ReVision, when the actual make and model may be changed, proofreading can only improve how well the car runs—or in this case, how well the writing works. This step fixes all the mechanics of writing:

Spelling

Sentence structure

Punctuation (commas, quotation marks, ending marks)

Capitalization

Again, students are given a copy to keep in their writer's toolkit. We are sure that by now you realize that our students receive copies of all the lists and charts so they can always have these tools readily available. It is also advantageous for the teachers to remind students of "rules and tools" by directing them back to their writer's toolkit when they get stumped. Often, reteaching is not necessary.

Spelling

Spelling is taught within the context of writing and word study. We use books such as *Words Their Way* (Bear, Invernizzi, Templeton, & Johnston, 2000), *The Spelling Book: Teaching Children How to Spell, Not What to Spell* (Rosencrans, 1998), and Rebecca Sitton's Spelling Sourcebook Series (Sitton, 2002). We view spelling as a subskill of writing, not necessarily as a subject unto itself. However, a focus on spelling can help students learn morphology. In addition, we ensure that students spell words correctly in published work and learn to spell high-frequency words as they write.

STUDENT VOICES

What's the most important thing you learned this year that helps you as a writer?

"How to use my writer's toolkit. And, I was introduced to the way you should write and how to use Gifts of Words: adverbs, verbs, punctuation, and quotation marks." —Katrina, grade 6

"Similes and metaphors help me as a writer because I never knew what they were before and now I do. I didn't know if things made sense before." —Nicole, grade 6

Thoughts to Ponder

We enjoy this troubleshooting part of our program: reading students' work, looking for the trouble spots and then trying to create a solution. Being in a teacher research group helps this process. It is much easier and far more fun if you have colleagues who can help you develop the "next best idea."

Teaching the tools of the trade is the component of our program that really helps students understand how to improve their writing. These are the skills and strategies they indicate that they did not know before entering our class, and why they say they learned so much from their year doing "all that language stuff."

———— ✳ ————

Chapter 7

Moving Toward Independence

Writing Poetry

My brain was pop-pop-popping when I was looking at those poems.
I never knew a poet person could do that funny kind of thing.
—Sharon Creech, *Love That Dog*

At this stage, your classroom is a beehive of reading and writing activities. Most students are beginning to feel that they understand the relationship between the two. The class books and scaffolded writing activities have paved the way for more independence in the writing program. Now is the time to extend students' understanding by concentrating on specific genres of writing. The next four chapters go into detail regarding ways to teach word consciousness within specific genres. The focus of this chapter is poetry.

Poems have a power of their own. When one of our group wrote her first poems, she wondered, Why is something so simply said, so emotional? It must be because there are no extra words to hide behind. In poems, every word counts.

Of all the genres, poetry is often perceived as the most difficult to teach. We may see ourselves as capable writers but not as poets. However, when we teach students to try different poetic forms, we have found that our own voices also seem to emerge through poetry. We learn alongside the students. By using the activities in this chapter, we have seen students grasp the power of choosing just the right combination of words to convey their emotions. We have heard them puzzle over the sounds of the words and carefully edit their choices.

In each case, we use published poems as either a demonstration or a model for student writing. There is a natural progression from playing with words in games and isolated activities to using words in a poetic form. We adore the book *Love That Dog* by Sharon Creech (2001) and use it to entice our students, especially boys, into writing poetry. Students often have preconceived ideas about what poetry is: they think it must always rhyme and that writing poetry is too difficult. Inviting a poet to the classroom to share their work is a way to disrupt the perception that poems are arcane, particularly if you can find a teenaged poet or a high school rapper who is willing to share his or her work and to talk about the word choices involved. We have been amazed at the poems some of our students, even eighth-grade boys, develop when they have the support to express their ideas through poems.

Saturating Students in Poetry

Each day, we begin our poetry sessions with the following poem. It becomes a signal or ritual that notifies our students that we will be gathering to read and write poems. The initial lessons focus mainly on reading and experiencing poems. We need to soak in the genre, marinating in the sounds and feel of poetry, before trying it on our own.

"I," Says the Poem
by Eve Merriam

"I," says the poem matter-of-factly,
"I am a cloud,
I am a tree.
I am a city,
I am the sea,

I am a golden
Mystery,"

But, adds the poem silently,
I cannot speak until you come.
Reader, come, come with me.

Some of Our Favorite Poets

Francisco Alarcon	Langston Hughes	Mary O'Neill
Maya Angelou	Ted Hughes	Michael Rosen
James Berry	Dennis Lee	Cynthia Rylant
Sheree Fitch	Lois Lesynski	Carl Sandburg
Paul Fleischman	Myra Cohn Livingston	Shel Silverstein
Robert Frost	Eve Merriam	Judith Viorst
Seamus Heaney	Lillian Moore	Janet Wong
Mary Ann Hoberman	Judith Nicholls	Kit Wright
Lee Bennett Hopkins	Jack Prelutsky	Jane Yolen

The poems we read and share come from a wide collection of poetry books, many of which are listed in our bibliography. We have found *Poetry Goes to School* (Barton & Booth, 2004) to be a very helpful resource. These experienced educators have collected poetry ideas over a lifetime of teaching, and we know that their ideas are classroom tested. They suggest looking for poems by the poet since poetry books tend to go out of print very quickly. Discovering a favorite poet allows you to look for his or her work in multiple anthologies, in libraries, and on Web sites by and about poets. (Please note that not all poems are suitable for classroom use.)

In the beginning, all that is expected is that everyone read lots of poems. Some days we ask students to share their favorite poem from that day's reading with a small group. Some days we read a descriptive poem, such as "Steam Shovel" by Charles Malam (in Prelutsky, 1983, p. 216), without giving the title, and ask students to illustrate it. Another day we might read a poem and ask them to figure out what the subject of the poem might be. Sylvia Plath's poem "Mushrooms" (1959) works well for this, as do two poems by Emily Dickinson, "Snow" and "Snake" (1994). We ask students in groups to select favorite poems and read them to the class, to choral-read poems, unscramble jumbled poems, and select their favorite from three or four projected onto the overhead projector. Students are encouraged to collect Gifts of Words and to find poems and songs they love, which they then record in their reading response logs. Their response logs begin to look like scrapbooks. Throughout this process, we ask questions and draw from students what they like and dislike—and why.

FROM READING TO WRITING

When we are ready to make the transition from reading to writing poetry, we use the same process that worked when we played with words to make class books. For instance, we introduce poetry by using a beautifully illustrated book such as *Hailstones and Halibut Bones* by Mary O'Neill (1961), which contains poems about color that are full of similes, metaphors, and personification. Integral to this process is the modeling provided by a published author, and the use of cooperative groups of students who work and share ideas together.

When this cherished book is introduced, we read several poems over a couple of days. Before reading each poem, we ask students to describe what a color smells, tastes, or feels like. Then we read the corresponding poem from the book.

Following the reading of each poem, we compare the author's work with the descriptions generated by the students. We use this as an opportunity to gently scaffold students' writing by talking about the poet's use of language. Part of the discussion involves identifying the similes and metaphors we like best as Gifts of Words and recording them (e.g., *Black is the darkest cloud in a thunderstorm*).

Then, groups each choose a color and brainstorm ideas and images for the poem, focusing on strong words and effective language. At the end of this process, they write a four- or five-line poem on chart paper. Each group then visits all the other groups and makes suggestions to help with revisions. Groups then return to their original chart and choose which changes to make.

The descriptive poems from each group are mounted and bound into a class book entitled *Colorful Language*. This publication becomes a classroom resource, part of our Bank of Powerful Language, to be drawn from as needed throughout the year.

Examples From a Class Book

Black is the space between bright shining stars.
Yellow is the color of happiness.
Orange is the fire in a fireplace on a cold winter night.

Students individually then choose a color and create their own poems, revising and crafting them to their satisfaction, with a good copy and an illustration at the end. At this point we do not ask them to produce anthologies of poems about color, or individual color books, because we want to leave this as a choice for later, when students assemble an anthology.

Using a Color Poem Frame

As an extension to the preceding activity, you may want to use a poem frame, such as the one developed by Donna Scott to use with her sixth through eighth graders. Frames such as this often help the students structure their ideas in a way that sounds like a polished poem. As above, several poems and excerpts with vivid imagery pertaining to color introduce the activity before the students, in small groups, choose a color and brainstorm items and emotions represented by that color. When students share their ideas and discuss, as a class, literal and figurative language used to describe those items and emotions, Donna stresses developing imagery through the use of strong adjectives. She then provides the following frame, which requires prepositional phrases with vivid imagery. A group poem is created as a model before students work in pairs and alone.

(Name color) _____	Red
(color) is _____	Red is the dark of the night sky,
The _____	The blood that pours out of me,
And _____	And the carcass of a wildebeest that the lioness kills.
It's _____	It's the fire ants at work,
A _____	A rose opening in the sun,
And _____	And leaves of Poison Oak hiding in the forest.
(rename color) _____	Red —Josh, grade 7

The key to success is practice, modeling, and repetition. First, students create one or two poems together, then they create group poems, and finally they develop four or five versions on their own. Having a Bank of Powerful Language to draw on helps even the most reticent student create a compelling poem.

Found Poems

Found poems are exactly what they sound like. They are poems that student writers create, or "find," while they are reading. Students create these poems by highlighting key words and phrases that capture the essence of the piece of writing. Found poems help us to focus on language use and vocabulary, especially with English language learners. This activity helps students pay attention to how individual words and phrases can convey meaning and also gives them a sense of the essence of a passage.

Guidelines for Developing Found Poems

- Any text, fiction or nonfiction, published or from the student's own writing, can be used. You can give students the text (e.g., Martin Luther King's "I have a dream" speech) or they can choose the text from which to create their poems.
- The original selection should be limited to a maximum of four pages and should contain interesting, descriptive, or provocative words.
- After reading the selection, have the students select a small number of phrases or words from the text. The number you choose will depend on the students and their grade. In fourth grade, using ten to twelve phrases works well.
- Each phrase must have fewer than four words.
- These words and phrases become the heart of the poem.
- Students can repeat phrases or words, modify the words slightly (change tenses, plurals, capitalization), and reorganize them as they wish.
- Each line should have no more than eight words.
- Vary the project by telling students to maintain the original order of the words or phrases, or not to add any words.
- After they have completed a first draft, ask students to think of a title and to recopy the words and phrases into a poetic form. Have students read aloud as they arrange the words on the page, paying attention to pauses, words they wish to emphasize, and spacing. If they type the poem, they can use boldface, italics, and different font sizes to create emphasis.
- Allow students to illustrate their poems if they enjoy doing so.
- At the bottom of the poem, cite the original source.

The poem in Figure 7-1, found in Martin Luther King's speech, captures some of the power of his speech and is a vivid way to honor his life in February, during Black History Month.

Fig. 7-1: "I Have a Dream" Found Poem

"I Am From" Poems

Another type of frame poem brings the student's home life more deeply into the class-room. Based on Linda Christensen's article about writing poetry that is culturally relevant in high school, this frame is simplified for upper elementary and middle school students (see Figure 7-2). However, it maintains the central purpose of bringing students' sense of self into the classroom.

> I am from cartoons on the T.V.
> rap music on the radio
> lamps hanging by chains
> and the soft brown couch in the living room.
>
> I am from a bike with no wheels in the backyard,
> The climbing tree reaching up to the sky,
> Beautiful red flowers
> And a park filled with graffiti.
>
> I am from spicy tacos,
> A sandía with chile and limón
> From tortas with jamón, queso, and jalapeños.
>
> I am from the black shoe box in the closet where
> I keep my money and old pictures of me.
> —Julio, grade 6

Note that the student didn't choose to include all the pieces from the framework in his final poem. The frame is a tool to help students if they need it, but it shouldn't become a con-stricting element.

Poetry Stations

To broaden students' experiences with writing different kinds of poems, we set up poetry-writing stations. Each station has a different short and simple writing activity to be completed. We organize our class into five groups and assign a poetry station to each group. Students rotate through each station, spending a day or two at each.

I am from _____ .
           (what you find around the house)

from _____ and _____ .

I am from _____ .
           (what you find outside the house)

I am from _____ .
           (describe what you remember of it using taste, touch)

I am from _____ and _____ .
           (something personal about you)

from _____ and _____ .
           (name people from your family or of the same heritage)

I'm from _____ .
           (list some sayings that are said in your family or characteristics about them)

and _____ .

from _____ and _____ .

I'm from _____

and _____ .

I'm from _____ and _____ .
           (name any legends or character names from stories)

_____ and _____ .

From the _____ .
           (use details from a famous story or incident in your family)

To the _____ .

Under my bed was

_____ .

I am from these moments —

_____ .

_____ .

Fig. 7-2: "I Am From" Poem Frame

Source: Adapted by Susana Herrera 6/01 from Linda Christensen, *Reading, Writing, and Rising Up* (2000)

STATION 1: SHAPE POEMS

Shape poems have words creating or outlining a visual image. They do not have to rhyme. These are the simple instructions:

Think of a favorite object or animal.

Draw the outline of the object or animal.

Brainstorm words related to the object or animal.

Arrange the words around the shape of the object or animal.

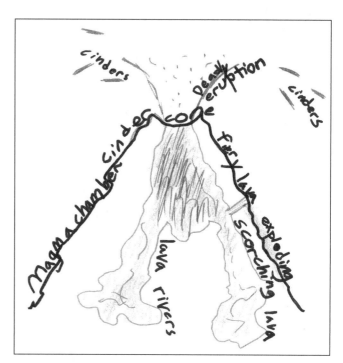

Fig. 7-3: Shape Poem

STATION 2: ACROSTIC POEM

Acrostic poems use each letter of a chosen word as the first letter for one line of a poem relating to that word. The word is then spelled vertically, like this:

Kaleidoscope of color

Across blue waters

Yearning to

Accelerate

Kingdom of waves

STATION 3: CINQUAIN

The cinquain is a simple five-line verse. To write one, choose a favorite object or person; then follow the frame.

Line 1: One-word title

Line 2: Two words that describe the title

Line 3: Three action words each ending with *-ing*

Line 4: Part of a sentence expressing a feeling

Line 5: One word describing or renaming the title

Here's an example:

Kittens
Frisky, playful
Mewing, jumping, bouncing
Creep silently on padded paws
Mischief

STATION 4: OPPOSITE POEMS

Another simple form for a poem is a diamond-shaped poem that starts with one concept (e.g., night) and ends with an opposite concept (day).

Line 1: One word—concept 1
Line 2: Two adjectives associated with concept 1
Line 3: Three verbs ending with *-ing* that describe concept 1
Line 4: Two nouns associated with concept 1, two nouns associated with concept 2
Line 5: Three verbs ending with *-ing* that describe concept 2
Line 6 : Two adjectives associated with concept 2
Line 7: One word—concept 2

For example:

Fire

Smoky, Hot

Burning, Flaming, Devouring

Houses, Trees, Fish, Lakes

Spraying, Shining, Sparkling

Blue, Cold

Water

STATION 5: HAIKU

Haiku is a very old and very short form of poetry that originated in Japan. Nearly every haiku is constructed of 17 syllables, divided into three units. The first section consists of five syllables, the second seven, and the last five again, although this pattern is not always strictly adhered to. Haiku captures a moment in time, usually from everyday life, and conveys it in exquisitely chosen language. Jan wrote this example for her class:

Summer rains falling
On the dusty garden and
A snail breathes again

Write a haiku about an everyday event. Follow the pattern of three lines divided into 17 syllables. The book *Red Dragonfly on My Shoulder* (1992), featuring haiku translated by Sylvia Cassedy and Kunihiro Suetake and illustrated by Molly Bang, is an excellent resource for this station.

SHARING CRITERIA FOR POETRY WRITING

In *Writing Anchors* (2004), Jan and her colleague Janine Reid provide a series of anchor lessons for writer's workshop that teach students to use their poet's eyes and ears to create original images. Students are encouraged to use their five senses and to play with language. Metaphor and simile are specifically taught, and students learn how poetry with voice and feeling can make an impact on the reader. Jan and Janine developed a set of criteria to share with students to encourage them to think deeply about the components of successful poetry. Working with rubrics really helps novice writers focus on what is essential. The Writing Profile for Poetry from *Writing Anchors* appears on the next page. It can be used to start conversations about the language of poetry.

FINAL ASSIGNMENT: ANTHOLOGY

Each student compiles a personal poetry anthology with a minimum of six poems he or she has written. The anthology must be in published form, meaning each poem must be word-processed or written in the student's finest printing, and each poem must be illustrated and mounted. The anthology must have a cover, a title page, and a page about the author. Students do not have difficulty finding poems to put in their anthology because they have written so many throughout this unit.

Although the poetry unit is now complete, this is not the end of poetry explorations for our students. They continue to read poems, and often choose to write poems in writer's workshop. Many of the ideas we introduce in this unit are repeated throughout the year. For example, after a class sleepover at the school and a day at the beach, the students wrote in their journals and then highlighted key words. These found words and phrases were assembled as poems and bound into a class book.

WRITING PROFILE FOR POETRY			
Dimensions of Writing	**Undeveloped—1** At a glance: Poem lacks originality; it is clichéd and fails to engage the reader.	**2-3-4**	**Fully Developed—5** At a glance: The poem engages the reader; it is original and creative.
Engagement with the topic • Meaning • Ideas • Details	Text may be unclear or illogical. There is little development of ideas. Writing lacks impact.		Poem conveys meaning clearly. Poem is fully developed in an unusual or original way. Writing creates an impact on the reader.
Vividness and language use • Energy • Passion • Voice • Word choice • Variety • Expressiveness • Originality • Creativity	Writing makes a stereotypical response to the topic; it may contain clichés. Writing lacks energy and personal engagement. The voice of the writer is unclear or generic. Writing lacks audience appeal in its current form. Language is simple. Originality is lacking.		Poem is highly individual and expressive. The writer expresses energy for the topic. Vivid language conveys meaning in the writer's own voice. Writing has audience appeal—would do well read aloud. Words are chosen for effect. The writer may experiment with poetic devices such as metaphor or simile. Sensory language is included. The writer takes risks to use language and expression in original ways.
Organization and structure • Sequence • Clarity • Focus • Cohesion	There is little or no introduction. Poem loses focus. Structure is difficult to follow. Poetic form is undeveloped. Pattern is simplistic and lacks impact. Ending may be abrupt.		Opening lines draw the reader in. Poem flows smoothly and seems cohesive; it is clear and sequential. Writing is easy to follow. Writer uses line breaks and white space to enhance the meaning. Phrases are varied in length. Pattern is chosen for effect. Poem ends with a satisfying conclusion.
Conventions • Spelling • Punctuation • Grammar	Frequent errors in spelling, punctuation, and grammar make the writing difficult to understand. Presentation lacks care.		Basic grammar, spelling, and punctuation are correct, but there may be some errors in complex structures.

Source: Wells & Reid (2004). Reproduced with permission.

Thoughts to Ponder

As Lucy Calkins (1986, 1994) points out, we need to teach students strategies to use over and over, not just impart a quick fix for a specific piece. To find poems that can be used as frames, we spend time reading and looking for pieces that speak to us. We think these finds will be different for different people. This is the key to using poems and books for your teaching. The particular book or poem is not as important as the passion and purpose each teacher brings to the activity. For example, while recently browsing through a stack of children's books, we came across the most wonderful find: *If Sarah Will Take Me* by Dave Bouchard. It is a poem/story about a paraplegic man who recalls his favorite places. The only way he can revisit them is "if Sarah will take me." We fell in love with this book and are confident that we can scaffold a writing experience based on it. We think you will soon find your favorites that offer your students ways to jump feetfirst into poetry. Of the many excellent resources available to support the teaching of poetry, we also have some favorites, listed in the box at right.

Professional Resources to Support the Teaching of Poetry

Barton, B., & Booth, D. *Poetry Goes to School*

Cullinan, B. E., Scala, M. C., & Schroder, V. C. *Three Voices: An Invitation to Poetry Across the Curriculum*

Heard, G. *Awakening the Heart: Exploring Poetry in Elementary and Middle School*

Ruurs, M. *The Power of Poems: Teaching the Joy of Writing Poetry*

Swartz, L. *Classroom Events Through Poetry*

Wells, J., & Reid, J. *Writing Anchors*

Chapter 8

Moving Toward Independence

Writing Memoirs

Writing is thinking. It is more than living,
for it is being conscious of living.
—Anne Morrow Lindbergh, *Locked Rooms and Open Doors*

When young writers begin to create longer stories, they run into a number of problems. They create characters who behave inconsistently or have no life at all. These characters crash from one (often violent) event to the next, for no apparent reason. The story endings rarely come to any logical closure. Word choice is often flat and lifeless. After much thought and reflection, we concluded that our students were not connecting their writing to their personal knowledge, so, of course, their words did not portray believable emotion. At that point, we decided to insist that, for a while, students could only write about their own lives. We chose a memoir unit as a way to focus on genuine emotion, and to help each student develop the language of his or her own voice.

The Writing Unit: Memoirs

Are we stifling students' creativity and imagination by assigning the topic? Well, to be perfectly honest, it seems more important to give them the tools they need to express ideas than to leave them writing imaginatively but with no thought for the needs of their readers. In doing this, we discovered that there are intermediate steps and scaffolding that help our young writers grow in skill and confidence. When they become thoughtful word choosers, they actually have the tools they need to write creatively and imaginatively.

The procedure we follow in our unit on memoirs will seem familiar. We introduce cherished books, discuss and examine how the books can be used to scaffold memoir writing, draft and share entries based on books read and personal experiences, work in groups, select pieces for publishing, revise, proofread, and publish.

USING PICTURE BOOKS TO STUDY THE GENRE OF MEMOIR

> *A genre study is a structure we create in order to scaffold and support reading-writing connections. Our students read and evaluate, muse over and analyze, learn from and model themselves after texts that are like those they will write.*
> —Lucy Calkins, *The Art of Teaching Writing*

We use picture books because they highlight family dynamics, childhood memories, special events, and relationships quickly and easily. We can also read one or two in each lesson. Students willingly read and reread these books simply because they can understand and enjoy the stories without the complexity that longer texts present. This allows all students to become more fully involved regardless of reading ability.

Once we collect our family of stories, we organize them into themes such as siblings and the problems they create, favorite things, pets, family stories, grandparents, and relatives. Each class begins with the reading of a picture book, followed by talk and storytelling, and ending with the students writing. We write with our class, sometimes on large chart paper, so they can witness our own struggles. Whenever possible, we share what and why we're writing by thinking aloud. As an end product, we publish a set of memoirs that they give to parents/guardians as a gift. By doing this, we try to make our exploration of memoirs as genuine as possible.

We begin this particular study with one of our all-time favorite books, *Wilfrid Gordon McDonald Partridge* by Mem Fox. It tells the story of a little boy who lives next door to a retirement center. The elderly residents become his friends, but Miss Nancy is his favorite. When he overhears his parents say that Miss Nancy has lost her memory, he tries to help her. As he gives Miss Nancy objects he has collected that match definitions of memory that he's been given (e.g., a memory is something warm), she begins to remember. A story such as this provides the perfect springboard to explore and write memoirs.

We follow this with *The Memory Box* by Mary Bahr, which tells the story of a lad spending his summer holidays with his grandparents. During this summer the boy and his grandfather begin to put items into a box; his grandfather has Alzheimer's disease so this becomes a way to collect and retain cherished memories. After reading these two books, we ask students to collect objects that are precious to them. Some students bring the objects to class and share the memory that makes each a treasure; others just recall and share. Students then write about these objects as a free-form narrative in either a writing folder or a writer's notebook (Calkins, 1986, 1994).

My Rotten Redheaded Older Brother by Patricia Polacco and *The Pain and the Great One* by Judy Blume are about siblings. Students love to listen to these books and then tell their own funny, silly, or sad stories about their siblings. After discussing and reading these two books, students are ready to write brief descriptions of funny or silly incidents in their families.

Next, we read Judith Viorst's *The Tenth Good Thing About Barney*, in which a boy recalls ten good things about his cat that had died. It provides a vehicle for students to discuss and tell stories about their pets. Again, we ask them to write a focused narrative using this writing prompt: "Write ten good things about a pet or someone in your life."

In the book *Guess Who My Favorite Person Is* by Byrd Baylor, the characters play a game of naming their favorite things. However, it is not acceptable to say that their favorite color is blue; they have to describe the kind of blue. A review of metaphors and similes using samples from the text helps students when they respond to this prompt: "List five of your favorite things, describing each as modeled in the book."

When I Was Young in the Mountains by Cynthia Rylant models how individual events can be assembled into one book. Before this lesson, we ask students to bring a photograph to class that will aid them in telling a story. After a small-group storytelling session, students respond to this prompt: "Write the story that goes with a photograph that you have brought from home."

James Stevenson's *When I Was Nine* is a collection of photographs and one-line memories. We discuss our favorite age and why, recalling significant events. Students then choose an age and list as many events or memories from that year as they can.

Relatives, family stories, and special events provide a wealth of writing ideas. *The Relatives Came* by Cynthia Rylant is an excellent scaffold for the prompt, "Write about one of your favorite relatives or your most hated relative." This is followed by Jane Yolen's *Owl Moon*, the story of a child and father looking for owls on a moonlit winter night, and Bill Martin and John Archambault's *Knots on a Counting Rope*, a story in two voices where a boy asks his grandfather about his birth. As we read and reread these books, students collect words, phrases, or sentences for the Bank of Powerful Language, such as *heart pounding afraid* (*Knots on a Counting Rope*) and *the snow below it was whiter than milk in a cereal bowl* (*Owl Moon*).

These are words and phrases that they think the author uses exceptionally well. We record these on strips of tagboard and add them to the Bank of Powerful Language. Then we ask students to tell, in their notebooks, special stories from their families or to write about a special event.

MODELING THE WRITING PROCESS

We also use these books as models for our own writing. Bonnie wrote the following story on the board, thinking aloud about her word choice and writing decisions as she did so.

Tell Me Again

Tell me the story, Nan.
Tell me again.
Your Great Uncle Charlie
was older than I.
Tell me the part about him teasing you.
Well, he would turn
the stair lights out…
Tell me why, Nan.
All us kids slept upstairs
and there was no electricity in our bedrooms.
So the only light was
in the stairs, right Nan?
That's right.
Tell me what he did, Nan.
He would lie down

on one of the steps.
Would he say anything?
No.
Would he move?
No.
Could you see him?
No.
Tell me what happened, Nan.
I would climb the stairs,
paying no attention.
Then what, Nan?
I would step upon
the step where he lay.
Did you scream?
Yes!
Did you faint, Nan?
Almost!
Were you terrified, Nan?
Always!
Did you still love him, Nan?
Of course.

When she finished, Bonnie read it to the class and asked, "What did I do as an author?" Their reply was that there was more than one person talking. From there, she was able to discuss the idea that *Knots on a Counting Rope* had provided a way to frame the piece—with the grandchild's request for a favorite story and his grandfather's responses—and to show how a piece of literature can scaffold writing.

At this point we ask students to spend three or four class periods reading and rereading our collection of memoir-type books (see page 133 and the bibliography) with a partner. We encourage discussion by asking, "Would this book qualify as a memoir? Why or why not?" After reading each book, partners generate writing ideas that are recorded on a class chart. They then choose topics to write about. For example:

- Your grandpa and what he likes to do
- Stories that a relative told you
- A special event
- A relative gave you something and told you a story about it
- Grandparents remember their "other" country
- Your pet
- A crazy, unusual relative
- A visit from your relatives
- A special place you love to visit

LOOKING AT LEADS

We also examine memoir-type books to generate a list of the leads specific to this genre, such as "I remember," "Once, when I was little," "One time, a long time ago," "In my family, we usually," or "I'm older now, but sometimes I look back and I remember." The students recognize these patterns and begin to use them in their own writing.

GETTING DOWN TO WRITING

We incorporated in our classrooms the notion of moving from daily writing folders to an author's notebook to capture ideas for memoirs (Calkins, 1986, 1994). Notebooks are very special. They are usually hardbound journals or decorated lined notebooks, depending on the wish of the student, where authors collect ideas for writing. Some ideas are random, some are lists, some are words or phrases, and others are kernels for stories. Students do not draft in their notebooks; instead, they use them to collect ideas. This is where we ask them to write excerpts related to writing prompts and to record observations. When it is appropriate, and enough excerpts and ideas have been generated, students identify seed ideas to develop into drafts that are kept in a separate writing folder. Whole entries or parts of entries can be chosen. In some cases, additional entries are written to enhance a particular focus. For example, a student who wants to use an entry about her grandmother may generate more ideas for entries about her grandmother. At this point, students think about the message that they want to communicate and the form that the message will take. Will it be a poem, or several poems? A letter? A short story? Students' memoirs take a variety of forms: poems, letters, stories, and short paragraphs, all developed from the entries in their writer's notebooks. Drafting begins, followed by revision, proofreading, and, finally, a published edition of each student's memoirs. The following examples illustrate the type of writing generated by this genre study.

Memoir-Type Picture Books

Ackerman, Karen, *Song and Dance Man*

Bahr, Mary, *The Memory Box*

Baylor, Byrd, *Guess Who My Favorite Person Is*

Blume, Judy, *The Pain and the Great One*

Dorros, Arthur, *Abuela*

Fox, Mem, *Shoes From Grandpa*

Fox, Mem, *Wilfrid Gordon McDonald Partridge*

Khalsa, Dayal Kaur, *Tales of a Gambling Grandma*

Martin, Bill, and Archambault, John, *Knots on a Counting Rope*

Nobisso, Josephine, *Grandpa Loved*

Pinkwater, Daniel, *Aunt Lulu*

Polacco, Patricia, *The Bee Tree*

Polacco, Patricia, *Chicken Sunday*

Polacco, Patricia, *Mrs. Katz and Tush*

Polacco, Patricia, *My Ol' Man*

Polacco, Patricia, *My Rotten Redheaded Older Brother*

Rylant, Cynthia, *The Relatives Came*

Rylant, Cynthia, *When I Was Young in the Mountains*

Say, Allen, *Grandfather's Journey*

Sheldon, Dyan, *The Whales' Song*

Stevenson, James, *When I Was Nine*

Viorst, Judith, *The Tenth Good Thing About Barney*

Yolen, Jane, *Owl Moon*

"Come on, the trailer's already packed," Dad yelled from downstairs. I opened my eyes and stared up at the rough, white ceiling of my room. The fiercely bright sunlight hinted, none too gently, that I should have been awake hours ago. The flaming sun seemed devoted to frying my glazed eyeballs with a concentrated beam of light. (Mareyn, grade 7)

Once, when I was ten, I had a surprisingly wonderful day at the beach. The golden sun dancing on the waves picked up my spirits. (Aaron, grade 7)

There are many wonderful picture books that can spark students' memories and serve as models for their writing. See the box for a few that we cherish.

SETTING CRITERIA FOR WRITING A MEMOIR

The following rubric is reproduced from *Writing Anchors* (Wells & Reid, 2004). We use it, and other rubrics, to help our students understand how to improve their writing.

WRITING PROFILE FOR PERSONAL MEMOIR			
Dimensions of Writing	**Undeveloped—1** At a glance: The writing is brief, hard to understand, and generic in tone.	**2-3-4**	**Fully Developed—5** At a glance: The writing is focused, expressive, easy to read, and original. Engagement with the topic.
Engagement with the topic • Meaning • Ideas • Details	Topic may be unclear or illogical; writing is brief with little development of ideas and few details or explanations.		Topic is focused and easy to read; the meaning is clear. Ideas are developed with relevant details, examples, and explanations. The writer expresses a strong point of view. Writing may include personal feelings and opinions.
Vividness and language use • Energy • Passion • Voice • Word choice • Variety • Expressiveness • Originality • Creativity	Writing provides stereotypical response to the topic and may contain clichés. The writer lacks energy and personal engagement. The voice of the writer is unclear and generic. Writing has no audience appeal in its current form. Language is simple. Writing lacks originality.		Writing is highly individual and expressive of the writer. The writer expresses energy for the topic. Rich and vivid language conveys details in the writer's own voice. The text has audience appeal—it would do well read aloud. Words are chosen for effect. The writer may experiment with poetic devices such as metaphor or simile. Sensory language is included. The writer takes risks to use language and expression in original ways.
Organization and structure • Sequence • Clarity • Focus • Cohesion	Writing has little or no introduction. Writing loses focus; it is difficult to follow. There is a simple, repetitive sentence pattern. Ending may be abrupt.		Writing begins with an arresting lead. Ideas are easy to follow and are cohesive. Writing flows smoothly; it is clear and sequential. Sentence length and pattern are varied. Writing has a satisfying conclusion.
Conventions • Spelling • Punctuation • Grammar	Frequent errors in sentence structure, spelling, punctuation, and grammar make the writing difficult to understand. Presentation lacks care.		Basic sentence structure, grammar, spelling, and punctuation are correct. There may be some errors on complex structures. Presentation shows care.

Source: Wells & Reid (2004). Reproduced with permission. (Adapted title.)

Personal writing demands strength and voice. Too often it is stereotypical and lifeless. Using the rubric Writing Profile for Personal Recounts provides an avenue for discussing ways in which students can improve their writing. For example, Bryan chose to write a letter as part of his memoir anthology.

> Dear Aunt and Uncle,
> Thank you for the game that you gave to me for my Game Cube. And thank you from my brother although he never plays because I always do. Once again thank you for everything you guys do for us. You are wonderful.
> Love Bryan (grade 6)

This piece could be strengthened by the addition of detail, explanation, and examples, all features that make personal writing richer. What does Bryan like about the game? Can he describe it to us? Why does Bryan's brother never get to play on the Game Cube? What does the brother think about this? What does he say? If Bryan includes more detail, which only he can know, the piece will be stronger.

Similarly, we want to know what other things this much-appreciated uncle and aunt have done for their nephews. Can Bryan remember another time when they did something for him? What are the details?

Using the rubric, we can show Bryan where his writing lacks strength and send him back to revise his letter, making it more detailed and thoughtful.

Give students copies of the rubric for their writer's toolkit. Ask them to use the rubric before presenting their first drafts. Have they done the best they can do to include rich detail and personal voice? Ask them to read their piece to a friend and see if the friend can suggest places where more detail is needed to paint a picture for the reader. Finally, you can use the rubric to assist in marking or grading the finished copy.

Thoughts to Ponder

The time of year this unit is taught seems to predict the degree of its success. At the beginning of the year, we encountered less success. Our students needed time and an accumulation of experiences before they could internalize the idea of using powerful language in their memoirs.

One of our initial assumptions was that having students write about what they know and have experienced would enable them to describe their stories well. We found that this was not true. Their experiences alone were not sufficient. They needed to become observers of their own actions. Using drama and discussing word choice helped them to actually see, for example, how people walk, and to conscientiously capture the movement with words. In addition, creating opportunities for them to record observations in their writer's notebook—things they noticed on the way home from school, at the dinner table, or while getting ready for a game— forced them to look anew at their daily lives and wonder about the small things they normally take for granted.

—— ✳ ——

Chapter 9

Moving Toward Independence

Writing Fictional Stories

I like the way people describe things, like the problem in the story.
I'm dying to know what's going to happen.
—Sophie, grade 6

Moving from poetry or memoir to another genre can lead in several directions. The most important point is to continue to scaffold students toward independent writing with powerful language use as a central theme. We moved toward writing longer stories to address some reoccurring problems in students' work, such as characters with no character, flat settings, and uninspired dialogue.

Reading Short Stories as a Springboard to Writing Fiction

Consistent with the other parts of this language-based program, the unit begins with the models that other authors provide, as students read short stories and examine the elements that make them effective. Short stories can be found in literature anthologies and in special collections. If only a single copy is available, a read-aloud works well to meet your needs. The key is to read these stories together and begin discussions on characters, settings, plots, endings, and mood. To supplement the short stories, picture books often provide excellent examples of each of the story elements you want to highlight, such as exciting lead sentences, rich character development, dialogue, and powerful words that the author uses to create vivid images (see the box for suggestions). Writing study groups, formed by students, help manage small-group discussions.

Suggested Picture Books for Highlighting Story Elements

Aliki, *Marianthe's Story: Painted Words, Spoken Memories*

Andrews, Jan, *The Very Last First Time*

Bridges, Shirin Yim, *Ruby's Wish*

Bunting, Eve, *Night of the Gargoyles*

Cameron, Ann, *The Most Beautiful Place in the World*

Cameron, Ann, *The Stories Julian Tells*

Cooney, Barbara, *Miss Rumphius*

English, Karen, *Nadia's Hands*

Fleischman, Paul, *Weslandia*

Heide, Florence Parry, and Gilliland, Judith Heide, *The Day of Ahmed's Secret*

Henkes, Kevin, *Chrysanthemum*

Lawson, Julie, *A Morning to Polish and Keep*

McGugan, Jim, *Josepha: A Prairie Boy's Story*

Smythe, Anne, *Islands*

Spalding, Andrea, *Solomon's Tree*

Steig, William, *Brave Irene*

Wiesner, David, *Flotsam*

Wild, Margaret, *Fox*

Yerxa, Leo, *Last Leaf, First Snowflake to Fall*

CREATING CRITERIA FOR SUCCESS

To develop the understanding of elements of short stories, students use the books they are reading to create individual lists of the elements that make a well-written story. Each group compiles the individual lists into a group list to be shared with the whole class. The class discusses the elements students have identified and develops a final class criteria list for a well-written story. Given the previous work in our classrooms, this list is thorough. The teacher can add ideas at this stage, ensuring that the qualities of a good narrative are brought forth. The following rubric is from *Writing Anchors* (Wells & Reid, 2004).

WRITING PROFILE FOR NARRATIVE			
Dimensions of Writing	**Undeveloped—1** At a glance: The story is brief, hard to understand, and unoriginal.	**2-3-4**	**Fully Developed—5** At a glance: The story is focused, expressive, and easy to read. It shows originality.
Engagement with the topic • Meaning • Ideas • Details	Text may be unclear or illogical. There is little development of ideas; text is predictable and lacking in originality. Writing does not engage the reader.		The meaning is clear; the story has a structure that the reader can follow. A problem is introduced and solved. Characters are developed and consistent. Detail is used effectively to create the setting and the mood.
Vividness and language use • Energy • Passion • Voice • Word choice • Variety • Expressiveness • Originality • Creativity	Writing lacks energy and personal engagement. Voice of the writer is unclear. Story does not engage the reader. Language is simple. Originality is lacking.		Original ideas may be developed in unusual ways. Rich and vivid language engages readers and keeps them interested. Words are chosen for effect; the writer may experiment with poetic devices such as metaphor and simile. Sensory language is included. Writing could be read aloud easily.
Organization and structure • Sequence • Clarity • Focus • Cohesion	There is no clear beginning, middle, and end. Writing loses focus and is difficult to follow. There are simple repetitive sentence patterns or poorly constructed sentences. Ending may be abrupt.		Writing begins effectively, flows smoothly, and is clear and easy to follow. Writing is cohesive and transition words used effectively. Sentence length and patterns are varied. Writing ends with a satisfying conclusion.
Conventions • Spelling • Punctuation • Grammar	Frequent errors in sentence structure, spelling, punctuation, and grammar make the writing difficult to understand. Presentation lacks care.		Basic spelling, punctuation, and grammar are correct. Presentation of writing shows care.

Source: Wells & Reid (2004). Reproduced with permission.

Bonnie's class came up with the following criteria to guide their story writing.

Criteria for a Well-Written Story

1. Use of powerful language
   - Show, don't tell
   - Gifts of Words
   - Similes
   - Convincing conversation or dialogue
2. An effective lead
3. Enticing, believable characters who are described in detail
4. Good plot (may not contain all elements)
   - Suspense
   - Exciting mystery
   - Romance
   - Heartwarming
   - Adventure and action
5. A good title that is not a label
6. A good ending, maybe with a twist
7. Creative, appropriate, well-described setting
8. Humor

Once the criteria are generated, each group rates five short stories. Each student then chooses his or her top three stories and explains why each is rated so highly. This is a great reading activity, as the students have to analyze the text and note great language, good leads, exciting features, strong characters, and so on. It really focuses their reading and, in the process, the criteria may be modified.

Writing Their Own Short Stories

Once the criteria are developed, we engage in a series of activities that focus on the development of story elements, such as character and setting, before students start drafting their stories.

CHARACTER DEVELOPMENT

When we read a particularly good description of a character, that character comes alive with mannerisms, attitude, and style that capture the essence of the person on the page. Bud from *Bud Not Buddy*, Alexander from *Alexander and the Horrible, Awful, No Good, Very Bad Day*, and Wilbur from *Charlotte's Web* are all prime examples of well-developed characters. Creating a believable character is an art, and the attention to detail required to paint a realistic picture of a character needs to be cultivated in students. We do this through a series of activities that add depth to a stock character so that students can experience the development of a nuanced description of a protagonist.

If students think and talk about a character, it becomes easier to develop a story around that person. We ask students to recall memorable characters from books they have read independently or heard read aloud over the years and discuss what is known about them. This may spill over into a discussion of the way characters are depicted in movies made from books. From that, we have students think about the type of story they wish to develop (e.g., science fiction, historical fiction, adventure) and brainstorm possible characters who might be found in these stories (e.g., a thief, an old sea captain, a murderer, an alien). As this happens, the students need to extrapolate the character type from the character (e.g., Harry Potter is *an adolescent wizard*). Each student then chooses one character and, through lots of discussion with their study group, gathers ideas about what this character might look and sound like and how he or she might behave. They then draw their characters and complete a character profile that includes age, nickname, height, hair color, and the like. To flesh out the character, they choose five of the following prompts and use their notebooks to draft ideas.

1. Write a background history.
2. List the character's favorite possessions.
3. Create a web of vocabulary words to describe the character's physical appearance.
4. Web vocabulary to describe the character's personality.
5. Dress up and interview each other "in character."
6. Write "a day in the life" of the character.
7. List the character's pet peeves.
8. List the character's wishes, beliefs, or dreams.
9. Who is the character's best friend? Write about meeting this best friend.
10. What makes the character happy, sad, fearful?

In these activities, students are challenged to create a character so real and so well developed that a story about that person just rolls off the pen. The intent is not to do all these activities but rather to pursue enough that students are "inside the head" of their character. When students see their character as a human being, with a personality, developing logical story events and deciding what their character will say and how he or she will act becomes an easier assignment. These activities all lead to the portrayal of a richly

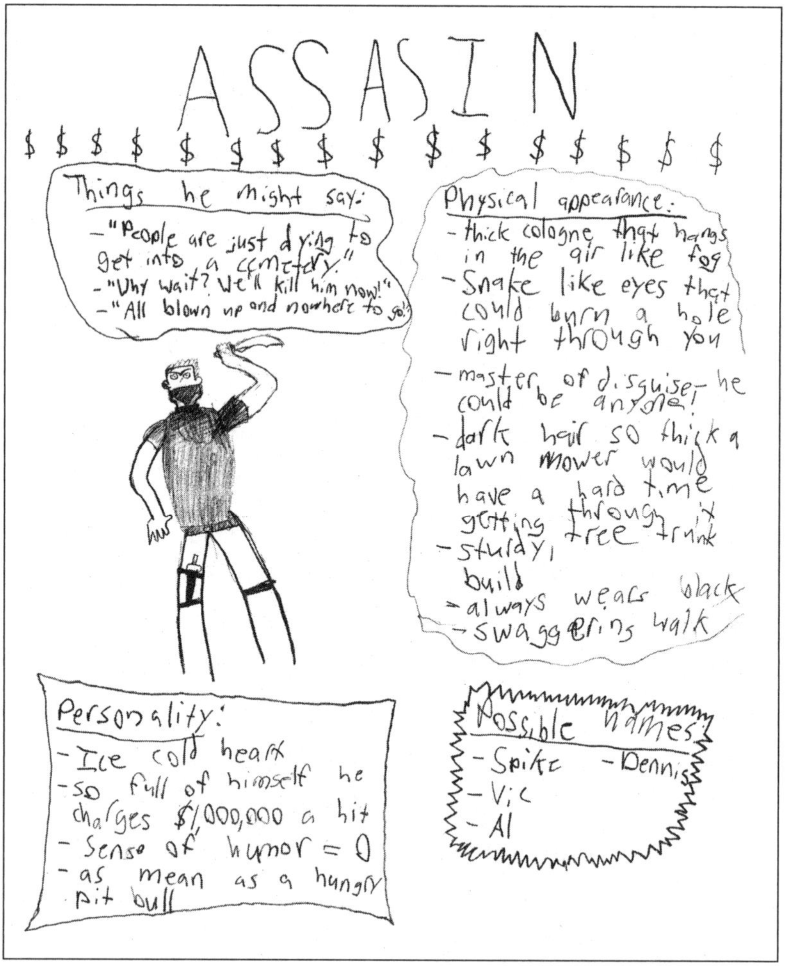

Fig. 9-1: Student Example of a Character Card

developed character. Students do not need to use these characters in a story, but the experience of understanding ways to develop and show personal characteristics in writing will facilitate their other writing.

Bonnie knew she was successful when, after she had given instructions, a student asked, "Do we answer what we think or what our character thinks?"

Information about each character can be summarized on a character card (see the student example in Figure 9-1 and the guidelines in Figure 9-2). Other students can then borrow a card when they want to introduce a similar character in their story. It gives them ideas that they can develop further on their own.

Character Card

My character is a (insert character type) _____

Age _____ Height _____

Possible Names _____

Nickname _____

Use rich vocabulary to describe your character's physical appearance.

Use rich vocabulary to describe your character's personality.

List some of the things you think your character would say.

List his or her favorite things.

Where would your character hang out?

Who/what would interact with your character?

Fig. 9-2: Character Card Guidelines

The Word-Conscious Classroom © 2008 by Judith A. Scott, Bonnie J. Skobel, and Jan Wells, Scholastic Professional.

DEVELOPING THE SETTING

A member of our teacher-researcher group, Alan Jones, who was working with younger students, developed this idea. He found that scaffolding the development of snippets of language was more effective with less skilled readers than trying to engage in writing of greater length. With shorter segments, he could focus the scaffolding of word choice directly, which enabled all the students to create sentences containing powerful language.

Setting cards are used to enhance the development of descriptive settings that match the characters. Once developed, they can be used by other students for ideas and in other stories. Here are the guidelines for this activity:

- The first step is to examine how established and published authors describe settings in the novels, picture books, and short stories the students are reading.
- As a whole group, discuss the effectiveness of these descriptions of settings. Identify what works to help the readers imagine the location and time frame of the story.
- Ask students to either draw a setting or find a suitable picture of a setting that is appropriate for their character—for example, an old sea captain would fit best on a ship or in a tavern, a ballerina might be found in a dance studio, and a space traveler could be on Mars. Old magazines can provide interesting settings.
- Do these next steps first with the class as a whole so you can model the process.
- Develop a chart like the one below (a big one for whole-class demonstration, and individual ones for the students). A blank form is provided in Figure 9-3.

2. Adjectives	1. Nouns	3. Verbs	4. Adverbs
fluffy foamy green majestic	cloud water mountain	floated crashing towering	lazily noisily silently

- Look at a picture and have students fill out the noun column first. Then, have them fill out the column with the descriptions of the nouns (adjectives). The order is reversed because adjectives usually precede nouns in sentences. Next, ask them about the verbs that *could* be associated with the nouns in the pictures, and finally, elicit descriptions of how the verb can act (adverbs). Leave plenty of space between the words and phrases.

Setting Card

Draw or look at a picture of a place.

- List the things you see in the picture under nouns in the second column.
- Next, fill in descriptions of the nouns (adjectives) in the first column.
- Next, list verbs that could be associated with the nouns in the pictures.
- Finally, write a description of how the verb could act (adverbs).
* Leave plenty of space between the words.
* After you have developed your chart, use it to write a few sentences to describe the setting.

2. Adjectives	1. Nouns	3. Verbs	4. Adverbs

Write the description of your setting using vivid language:

Fig. 9-3: Setting Card Guidelines

- After you have collected the words, use them to write a few sentences to describe the setting, using the chart as a springboard.

- When students do this, it works well to have them work in small groups. This can support word learning for English language learners.

- After students have discussed and charted the words, have them write a few sentences to describe the setting; for example, "The fluffy cloud floated lazily by the majestic mountains towering above the silent town."

- Ask the students to peer-edit the descriptions and then write the final descriptions on the backs of the pictures.

- You can leave the setting cards on a board or in a file for students to use when they are trying to write a scene and need some additional ideas or words.

DRAFTING THEIR STORIES

To help students organize their thoughts before they actually begin to draft their stories, we use a storyboard that highlights the criteria of a good story as generated by the students. This is much like the storyboards used in the movie business to sketch scenes briefly in words. As shown in Figure 9-4, it provides a concise and focused plotline and emphasizes elements students might neglect, such as lead, ending, and an interesting title. During this process, we encourage writers to discuss their story's development with their study group. They help each other determine problems that their characters might encounter, the setting of the story, and events that occur along the way.

Once the storyboard is complete, students present their stories to their classmates either orally or through drama. Presenting their stories in this way can encourage students to revise elements before the story is even written. This is also when students experiment with possible word choices. Students are often overheard discussing which Gifts of Words would work best, what their character should do next, how to make a particular part funny, which title to choose, how to spell a word, and how to end their story.

The effort and thinking that go into these storyboards make students eager to draft their stories. They now have the tools they need to soar. At this point, some students will write nonstop for three hours while others may take weeks to complete their drafts. We've seen drafts ranging from half a page to 108 typewritten pages after this process.

Title: (that grabs attention)	My main character:	Words and phrases I want to use:	
Setting:	Problem:	Moral: (lesson to learn)	My lead:
Beginning:	Action:	Action:	Action:
Action:	Action:	Action:	Ending:

Fig. 9-4: A Storyboard for an Adventure Story

REVISING THEIR STORIES

As students complete their first drafts, they meet with a partner or their study groups to read and revise their stories. Clean drafts are typed using computers as much as possible. Students are much less reluctant to change their stories if they don't have to rewrite them by hand. Each story is then photocopied three times and randomly passed out to other members of the class, who then begin to read and rate others' stories using the list of criteria already generated (see "Criteria for a Well-Written Story" at the beginning of the chapter) and a five-point rating scale. It's important to remind students that their role in this process is not that of a critic but of a caring editor.

Rating Scale Generated by Students

4   Extremely effective—WOW!

3   It works but doesn't blow my socks off.

2   It's OK but could be improved.

1   It's there but it just doesn't work or needs more detail.

0   Not there yet.

A copy of each story is handed to the managing editor (the teacher) for further revision through conferencing and proofreading. We also encourage students to solicit the help of their parents and to make use of spell-check on the computers for proofreading.

Upon receiving a minimum of three rating sheets and engaging in a brief writing conference with the teacher, students begin another round of revision. How each author chooses to alter the piece is his or her responsibility, but a low rating on story elements gives a writer valuable feedback for improvement. Finally, a revised copy is ready for publication.

PUBLISHING THEIR STORIES

Students are given a choice of how to bind and publish their stories. The easiest way to find interesting ideas is to explore the Internet. A book that we found very useful is Carol Wingert's *The Book Book* (2004). There are many ways to bind the pages, and we encourage students to be creative.

One of the easiest ways to publish a book is to use recycled file folders and copier paper. Fold the paper in half to form 8½" x 11" sheets. (If you're recycling used paper, fold the printed side to the inside; you'll be using only the outside of each sheet.) Separate the sheets. With the folded sides to the opening, insert the sheets into the center of the file folder. Staple through the file folder and the open edges of the paper to create a booklet where each folded sheet forms two pages of the booklet. Trim the folder to fit around the pages with a half-inch overlap. Cover the staples with colored masking tape and have students decorate the cover. They can either glue their typed work onto the pages or create the pages on the computer before they are stapled together. (This is quite a bit more difficult.)

Hardbound books can be created from cardboard and material scraps or purchased as blank books from several different companies. Bare Books, from Treetop Publishing, are inexpensive and easy to use.

ILLUSTRATING THEIR STORIES

If you can cultivate a relationship with an art teacher, illustration techniques can be taught in art class. If you provide your own art lessons, you can do these lessons yourself. Early in the year, we teach different kinds of lettering. We bring lettering books to use as samples in matching lettering to the topic. For example, if the word is *forest*, the letters can be drawn to look like twigs or trees. We provide scissors with fancy edges and scalloped rulers to teach different techniques for making borders. One art assignment is to design four title pages using four different topics, borders, types of lettering, and styles.

Illustrations can emerge from many of the techniques in the art curriculum, such as pencil sketching, tissue paper designs, torn-paper pictures, black pen drawing, watercolors, and collages.

And during drawing sessions, we emphasize different camera angles and perspectives. Zoom close-ups, views from below the picture, bird's-eye views, moving away and coming closer, double-page spreads, and panoramic views are all taught and used. Most of these perspectives and techniques can be found in the illustrations of picture books, and we encourage our students to look to these as models. Searching through picture books to find new and different perspectives can be great fun.

STUDENT VOICES

What does someone have to do in order to be a good writer?

"You need to read books on the things you want to write about."
—Michael, grade 6

"Learn how to write so the reader has pictures in their mind."
—Alexi, grade 6

"Some writers see something that is an inspiration, like a movie. You could use some of the characters in your own story."
—Luis, grade 6

What is the most important thing you learned about being an author?

"I learned to express my feelings with powerful language."
—Aman, grade 6

"I learned to use similes and metaphors." —Taylor, grade 6

"I learned to begin my stories with good leads." —Mireya, grade 6

"I learned that being a writer is hard, and I know how authors feel when they write." —Pavel, grade 5

"I learned that powerful language is what makes a reader want to read more." —David, grade 6

SHARING THEIR STORIES

An integral part of publishing a story is sharing it with an audience. Sharing can range from reading stories to a small selected group to reading to the full class, to other classes in the school, to trusted others at school and at home, or to a crowded room during a literacy night. What is important is that these stories are shared and appreciated by others.

How about just a 5th grade event - invite families - just do it at grade level.

Thoughts to Ponder

Producing a longer story is a major accomplishment for both students and teachers. In most cases, this unit of work fits best after spring break. It can be the culminating event of your writing program, when your students bring together all the hard work and learning they've engaged in throughout the year. Students will feel like real authors and be proud of their accomplishments.

— ❋ —

Chapter 10

Developing Word Consciousness Across the Curriculum

Until now, our focus has been, by and large, on reading and writing in a narrative style. However, once students leave school, they are likely to spend more time reading and writing nonfiction materials than reading or writing stories (Mikulecky, 1981). This means that paying attention to word consciousness across the curriculum is an important component of a word-conscious classroom.

Vocabulary learning takes on a slightly different slant when we focus on reading and writing about factual information. The types of words used in informational texts are often labels for important concepts, and each content area contains its own specialized collection of terms. Thus, words such as *tropical*, *ecosystem*, *diversity*, *canopy*, *vegetation*, *torrential*, and *organisms* are found on an introductory page of an informational book about the jungle (Greenaway, 1994). Often, other words, such as *because*, *furthermore*, *however*, *in conclusion*, *thus*, and *to summarize*, signal structural elements in informational texts. In addition, many of the words used in informational texts are defined either explicitly or implicitly within the text. By comparison, narrative texts tend to emphasize descriptive words related to characterization, setting, and tone.

The many different meanings of the same word can complicate the issue. However, as we mentioned in Chapter 1, building word schemas occurs when words are seen and heard multiple times in multiple contexts. This is one of the best reasons we know to teach students integrated units. Throughout this book, we have used a similar framework to concentrate on word consciousness. We now expand this frame with examples from social studies and research writing.

Using a Content-Specific Word Bank

The development of a content-specific word wall mirrors the development of the Bank of Powerful Language, although the context is more circumscribed. Its purpose is to nurture students' curiosity, love, and appreciation of words, increase their metacognitive awareness of how words are used in a particular genre, and develop their voice and style as writers. The content-specific word bank becomes a shared point of reference in an inquiry-based approach to the content area. The word bank is organized by characteristics that constitute the craft of writing within the genre that is being studied.

Organizing categories and parts of speech through color coding helps students use the bank along with supporting their developing understanding of grammar and morphology.

COLONIAL JOURNAL WRITING UNIT—FIFTH GRADE

This example comes from a unit of study designed by fifth-grade teachers (Tatiana Miller, Stu Branoff, and Laura Molanchon) at Bay View Elementary in Santa Cruz, California, in which students study historical fiction, the American Revolution, colonial times, elements of a narrative, and writing in a journal format. The diaries and textbook are read both together and independently in class. As they read or listen, students scrutinize the texts for words that could be useful, accurate, and descriptive when they write their final assignment—an imaginary journal set during the American Revolution.

Touchstone Texts for the Unit

Denenberg, Barry, *The Journal of William Thomas Emerson: A Revolutionary War Patriot*

Gregory, Kristiana, *The Winter of Red Snow: The Revolutionary War Diary of Abigail Jane Stewart*

McGovern, Ann, *The Secret Soldier: The Story of Deborah Sampson*

Moss, Marissa, *Emma's Journal: The Story of a Colonial Girl*

Word Bank for Colonial Times

This word bank is established, much like the Bank of Powerful Language, through capturing words during reading. They are then organized on the whiteboard according to the following categories.

SETTING

Setting words are printed on blue card stock and grouped together. All are nouns from that time period.

Harbor	Field	Marsh	Commons	Village	Meadow	Ridge
Cottage	Brick	Kettle	Hearth	Loom	Tavern	Oil lamp

CHARACTER

Character words are printed on yellow card stock and grouped together. All are adjectives, using shades of meaning, that could describe the characters in their story and prompt students' thinking about how their characters look and act, and how their appearance might convey aspects of their personalities.

Mighty	Muscular	Determined	Afraid	Terrified	Gigantic	Enormous
Skinny	Slender	Petite	Puny	Lanky	Noble	Confident

PLOT

Plot words are printed on green card stock and grouped together. All are verbs that represent different actions that could take place in the story. The verbs are specific to types of actions that are likely or consistent with wartime during the American Revolution.

Content-specific word banks can be adapted to any grade, content and type of writing assignment. Their use across the curriculum reinforces awareness of word use in all communication.

Deceive	Pretend	Hide	Surprise	Attack	March	Gallop
Warn	Refuse	Backstab	Rescue	Discover	Prevent	Save

Developing Persuasive Prose

Keeping a focus on word choice may seem difficult when dealing with nonfiction as a genre. The following entertaining idea for developing persuasive prose, adapted from Donna Scott, a teacher at North Woods School in Redding, California, builds on the food interests of middle school students.

After brainstorming favorite foods and restaurant words, students read excerpts from magazines such as *Bon Appétit* and several restaurant menus. They then work with partners to develop different categories of food words: verbs for cooking (e.g., *bake*, *fry*, *broil*, *steam*, *dice*, *chop*) and words that capture textures (e.g., *crunchy*, *chewy*), tastes (e.g., *salty*, *sweet*, *spicy*), and appearance (e.g., *smothered*, *layered*, *topped*).

Food photos cut from magazines are given to students to describe, alone or in pairs. The students' task is to entice a reader to eat in their new restaurant, using at least one adjective per ingredient. Final versions are shared aloud and posted with the pictures. Following is the piece produced by Tyler, an eighth grader.

Tiller & Peeker's Restaurant

Welcome to Tiller & Peeker's Dive-In Sundaes! Today's special is Lemon Custard Deep-Dish pie served with rich whipped cream swirled around the rim. It is topped with the finest handpicked lemon slices, surrounded by dollops of more whipped cream. The crust is baked to perfection, to our customers' standards. If this doesn't satisfy your taste buds, have a go at our scrumpdidilyumptious Pumpkin pie, topped with a layer of sweet cinnamon powder.

Freshly baked, these delicious pies are bound to make your taste buds go wild!

Research Writing

The Internet has exploded in the past decade, providing an incredible array of information at students' fingertips. In 2006, the Internet had 100 million Web sites. This is both exciting and daunting, as students need to learn how to evaluate, sort, and organize the information they find. Teachers often lament that students just download pages of information or cut and paste it directly from the screen. The prevailing attitude seems to be that information found on the Internet must be true and it's free for the taking, with no author attached. We need to disrupt this pattern and explicitly teach students how to conduct appropriate research investigations and how to write in a research genre.

STEPS IN THE RESEARCH WRITING PROCESS

The following steps help students develop a strategy for creating reports in any subject.

Choose a Topic

Either student- or teacher-selected topics can be used. If you are just introducing the process, assigning topics works well since you can limit the scope of the assignment. As students assume responsibility for choosing their own topics, they will need to learn how to narrow them to a manageable size.

When students begin to select research topics, they should start with topics that interest them or pique their curiosity. However, it's useful to choose three or four possibilities, because research material may be less available than expected for some topics. Then have students conduct preliminary searches for each topic. This can be done easily on the Internet. Students pick one of the topics that they think will be relatively easy to research over the days and weeks to come.

It's also important to help students determine whether the information they are gathering is from reliable sources. This can be done through a class discussion regarding the types of organizations posting the material. If the information comes from a museum site or a national center, it is more likely to contain accurate information than a personal blog.

Gather Facts

The first step in any research project is gathering facts. This is not an automatic process. It needs to be taught through demonstration and modeling. Show students how to take notes with lots of modeling. An easy way to do this is to have your whole class work from the same few pages of research, making sure the vocabulary is not too difficult. It is at this point that you introduce the fact sheet, which is simply an 8½" x 11" piece of paper divided into several rows and two columns, labeled Fact and Source.

The size of the boxes on the sheet depends on your grade and the corresponding size of your students' handwriting. The boxes should be big enough to accommodate student handwriting and small enough to discourage students from copying whole sentences. The task is to find and record important or interesting facts, key words, and phrases, using a maximum of eight to ten words. Each fact is written in a separate box; the source column tracks the page and book or Web site. Several sheets can be used as necessary. The idea is to have students gather facts without trying to immediately categorize them.

Sort Facts

After students have gathered facts from the source material, they need to organize them. This is an important step toward acquiring facility with academic writing styles. Scissors come out and the fact sheets are cut up into individual boxes. Be forewarned that this stage can be messy! The students sort the facts into categories and assign each category a heading.

In the beginning, when the whole class is working on the same project and has collected notes and facts together, the teacher models the process. However, before we even begin to sort facts, we develop the concept by sorting all types of objects, including shoes, buttons, and words. For instance, we put a group of words on the overhead and have students categorize them as a quick "sponge" activity. Sorting many different items creates an awareness of similarities, differences, and various ways to categorize objects, information, and ideas.

Sequencing Facts and Ideas

Now that the facts are categorized with headings, they need to be arranged in some order. Students can order them from most important to least important ideas, into related concepts, or into another logical sequence. Once a category is ready, the fact boxes are glued onto either a fact organizational sheet (shown in Figure 10-1) or into a notebook. This becomes the outline for their writing.

Writing Paragraphs

At this point, the majority of the work has been done. In the past, writing the paragraphs always seemed difficult. Now, for example, if the students have ten facts under the head-

Fig. 10-1: Fact Organizational Sheet

ing "Habitat," they will have ten facts for a habitat paragraph. You may need to teach students about opening and closing sentences for paragraphs and reports. However, you can use the same techniques we discussed in narrative forms of writing to develop interesting lead sentences and to conclude their essays.

Once students begin writing their facts into sentences, you can encourage them to go beyond the bare bones of the outline and elaborate their report with rich and powerful language. They can combine sentences, insert descriptive language, and practice creating the tone found in the original sources. They may also want to change the order of the facts. Renumbering the fact boxes with the desired order eliminates the mess of regluing. Draft copies of the emerging report may be kept in folders gathered by the teacher or written beside the facts in a notebook.

Assembling the Report

Before the report is complete, take students to the library to explore how other authors create a title page and/or book cover. Use these same books to teach what a table of contents looks like, how illustrations are used, how to use graphs and tables, and how the resources are listed. Students are now ready to produce a final publishable copy and to assemble their report.

EYEWITNESS PAGES

After years of wearily reading and marking research reports, we discovered an alternative that works with collaborative groups and provides a more interesting presentation. While we believe students need to learn how to create research reports, the results do not always need to look the same. We found that eyewitness-type books (published by DK Publishing) can be used as a model or pattern for presentation once the research is complete. For instance, an eyewitness atlas can serve as the model for presenting research information on individual countries. A map of a country is placed in the middle of each large atlas sheet covering a two-page spread. Surrounding it are five or six paragraphs related to the country with pictures attractively mounted among the paragraphs. The national flag is displayed in a corner and the entire sheet is bordered by an appropriate design.

Students follow the research-writing process outlined earlier, and when they are ready to assemble their reports, they are given a large sheet of tagboard. Attention is paid to the color scheme that would be appropriate for the chosen country. Students make a border that match-

Fig. 10-2: Eyewitness Page

es some aspect of the culture and print a map of their country for the middle of the page. The paragraphs and pictures are mounted on colored paper and artistically arranged. The finished products are displayed for all to see. Figure 10-2 shows one student's pages from a research project on ocean animals.

Creating Criteria for Success

Nonfiction writing and reports can be evaluated on several levels. In the rubric for nonfiction reports (from Wells & Reid, *Writing Anchors*, 2004), the focus is on dimensions of writing.

EVALUATING EYEWITNESS PAGES

To evaluate the report-writing process and the completed eyewitness page, we rate dimensions of design as well as dimensions of research, writing style, and conventions (see the rubric on page

RUBRIC FOR NONFICTION REPORTS			
Dimensions of Writing	**Undeveloped—1** At a glance: The report is brief and hard to understand, with loosely connected ideas.	**2-3-4**	**Fully Developed—5** At a glance: The report is focused, expressive, clear in intent; it effectively accomplishes the purpose.
Engagement with the topic • Meaning • Ideas • Details	Report may be unclear or unfocused and is difficult to follow. Purpose is vague. Information may be copied or inaccurate. Details are irrelevant.		Report is focused and clearly directed toward the purpose. Information is accurate and complete. Details support the main ideas and are used with intent to inform and clarify.
Vividness • Energy • Passion • Voice • Word choice • Variety • Expressiveness • Originality • Creativity	Writing lacks energy and evidence of personal engagement with the topic. Voice of the writer is unclear. Language is simple. Technical terminology may be absent or inaccurate.		Language is clear and precise, using accurate terminology when appropriate. Ideas are presented with voice and style. Words are chosen for effect. Technical terminology is used accurately and with effect.
Organization and structure • Sequence • Clarity • Focus • Cohesion	Writing may lack a clear introduction to the topic or conclusion. Report has simple, repetitive sentence patterns or poorly constructed sentences. Text features (headings, diagrams, graphics, etc.) are absent or used inappropriately.		Report begins with an arresting lead, flows smoothly, and ends with an effective summation of the information. Writing is clear and sequential. Writing is cohesive and shows clear, logical sequence and paragraphing. Text features (headings, diagrams, graphics, etc.) are used effectively.
Conventions • Spelling • Punctuation • Grammar	Frequent errors in sentence structure, spelling, punctuation, and grammar make the writing difficult to understand. Presentation lacks care.		Basic spelling, punctuation, and grammar are correct. Presentation of writing, graphics, and illustrations shows care. Special features make the report interesting to the reader.

Source: Wells & Reid (2004). Reproduced with permission.

RUBRIC FOR EYEWITNESS REPORTS			
Dimensions of Interest	**Undeveloped—1** At a glance: The artwork is messy. The paragraphs are inaccurate or brief and hard to understand.	**2-3-4**	**Fully Developed—5** At a glance: The artwork is attractive and the paragraphs contain well-written, factual material.
Dimensions of design	There are few pictures. Little attention is paid to elements of layout and design. Presentation lacks care.		Pictures are accurate and detailed. Borders are straight and decorative. The report is neatly and brightly colored. Layout and arrangement are eye-catching. Special features make the report interesting to the reader. Presentation of writing, graphics, and illustrations shows care.
Dimensions of research	There is little evidence of gathering or sorting facts. Information may be copied or inaccurate. The report doesn't capture important pieces of information. Details given are irrelevant.		There is strong evidence of gathering and sorting facts. Information is in student's own words. Paragraphs focus on important or interesting elements. Information is accurate and complete.
Dimensions of writing style	Paragraphs may be unclear or unfocused. Writing lacks energy and evidence of personal engagement with the topic. Text features (headings, diagrams, graphics, etc.) are absent or used inappropriately.		Writing is cohesive. Language is clear and precise, using accurate terminology when appropriate. Information is presented with style. Words are chosen for effect. Technical terminology is used accurately and with effect. Text features (headings, diagrams, graphics, etc.) are used effectively.
Conventions • Spelling • Punctuation • Grammar	Frequent errors in sentence structure, spelling, punctuation, and grammar make the writing difficult to understand.		Basic spelling, punctuation, and grammar are correct.

160). Criteria for all parts of the process are developed through discussion with the class. Then, as students glue down their facts and write their draft copies of the paragraphs, evaluation begins. Both the teacher and the student evaluate their work. These rating "marks" are recorded and notes about the student's ability to work with this process are recorded. Over time, students learn to self-evaluate wonderfully well, which keeps the teacher from having to "mark" everything!

The first time a class produces eyewitness pages, we talk as a class about the work and learn techniques from each other. We have found that this is a valuable process, particularly if students produce other products in this format.

Thoughts to Ponder

If research writing is started in the primary grades, then the older students will have internalized this process and will do it automatically. If not, don't despair—just roll up your sleeves and begin. Older students and their teachers often feel that cutting and pasting the facts really is not necessary. We disagree completely. Yes, they may be able to internalize this more quickly, but this is useful for all students. High-achieving students who often think that more is better need to learn to become more discriminating about the facts they collect. As they develop their reports, encourage students to discard facts that do not fit or don't make sense within the overall structure.

Students who use this process become more focused as research writers. We know university students who wish they had been taught this method and immediately adopt it. For the student who struggles with nonfiction and research writing, this method is invaluable. As the teacher, you can actually identify where the difficulty arises and can scaffold their learning either by teaching the skill or bridging to the next. When students create eyewitness pages, they love the fact that although they may not be great research writers, they can still produce an aesthetically pleasing report. Students who rarely hand in their work seem to thrive when given the opportunity to produce eyewitness pages.

—— ✳ ——

Chapter 11

Assessment and Evaluation

W hen students hand in a published book of their writing, we do not evaluate it by giving a mark out of ten nor do we assign a letter grade to the quality of their writing. We celebrate their accomplishment and award an embossed "Young Writer's Award" gold seal that is glued to the inside of their published work. Students share, as authors, with small groups, with the full class, and with other classes. In doing so, they take the very personal risk of opening up to others. Backward planning allows us to think about the end goal we desire for our students: we want them to develop into effective authors with a feeling of freedom and the knowledge that their audience will accept what they write and appreciate the stage of development that each published piece represents. Having said that, do we collect marks and make decisions about their writing for feedback and reporting purposes? As you can see from the rubrics embedded throughout the book, it's obvious that we do. However, this chapter goes into the rationale and development of rubrics in more depth, and presents a rubric for assessing word consciousness.

Assessing Student Work

Assessing refers to our ongoing observations of students' daily work and their writing projects in process. We keep a binder with two to three pages per student where we record our observations about their daily work. We record spelling errors that represent recurrent patterns for further focus; grammatical and word usage problems; areas they consistently have mastered (e.g., use of quotation marks, characters descriptions, effective leads); work-habit comments; notes from writing and reading conferences; use of time; and anything else that will help us form a picture of each student as a learner.

We also try to figure out students' developmental level of writing and record it. The first chapters of Lucy Calkins's *The Art of Teaching Writing* (1986, 1994) have been an invaluable reference. It is in these chapters that she describes in detail how schoolchildren develop as writers. Using these guides, we can determine why our sixth graders write the way they do and, more important, what they need next in order to develop. We are constantly observing and trying to determine each writer's zone of proximal development.

Some of us use sticky notes to record our observations and then later transfer them to our binders. This way we avoid the problem of having to rewrite information because we've left our binders somewhere else. By using the sticky notes, we eliminate at least one excuse for delaying our marking. While we record our observations for each student, we also keep a master list of students who have similar problems. Then, when we recognize, for instance, that two or three students need a lesson on the use of commas, we will gather them together and teach that lesson.

Evaluating Students' Work

We define evaluation as the process of judging a student's work and assigning a mark, a rating, or a letter grade. We mark students' simile cards (Chapter 7), character cards (Chapter 9), Show, Don't Tell cards (Chapter 7), literature circle participation (Chapter 6), note taking (Chapter 10), and tests, but *never* their final, best-I-can-do, this-is-who-I-am, for-the-world-to-read published writing.

The most effective method for us, and the one we use most often, is a rating scale or a rubric that identifies what we value in students' work. A gymnast, an ice skater, and a ballroom dancer all know what the judges are looking for in competitions. They look at style and form, defined in particular ways. These are the elements the performers focus on in practice. In the same way, students need to know how they are being judged and the criteria for their performance. This gives them insight into the elements that must be the focus of their attention. Knowing the criteria takes the mystery out of evaluation and helps all students, especially those who may not have the background knowledge to be aware of this on their own, know the bar they need to reach for particular marks. Since we value revision and redrafting, students always have the option of revising their work for higher marks.

To open up the process even further, we use student input to develop the criteria for marks, ratings, or letter grades. This helps students develop a metacognitive awareness of how marks are assigned and a sense of ownership over the process. They use the rubrics to self-assess their work and eventually develop a sense of responsibility for the quality of their work in these genres. It is important that students learn to see the elements of style in their own writing and to try to read it with another reader's eyes. By focusing on elements of clear, precise, book-style writing, our students understand how to hear, read, write, and live that language.

USING A WORD-CONSCIOUSNESS RUBRIC

Throughout this book, we have presented several activities to develop word consciousness. Although each activity can be evaluated separately, the metacognitive awareness of words that you develop, the excitement and enthusiasm for word choice, and the commitment to communicating in the style of "book words" are also worth capturing. This rubric can be integrated into others and can also be used alone. By using it to assess success in all written work, you will up the ante of word consciousness in your classroom.

RUBRIC FOR WORD CONSCIOUSNESS			
Dimensions of Word Awareness	**Undeveloped—1** At a glance: The student shows little curiosity or interest in words and only minimal growth in vocabulary acquisition.	**2-3-4**	**Fully Developed—5** At a glance: The student is curious and interested in words and shows evidence of continuous vocabulary acquisition.
Engagement with the topic • Enthusiasm • Risk-taking • Originality	The student shows little interest in word-awareness activities. In writing, there is little evidence of new word learning or risk-taking to try new ideas. The student shows little originality in word usage. The student lacks awareness of the role of vocabulary in the communication of ideas.		The student is fully engaged with word-awareness activities. In writing there is evidence of risk-taking to try new ideas. The student uses words in original ways. The student is aware of the role of vocabulary in the communication of ideas.
Word consciousness in reading • Engagement • Understanding • Attention to detail	The student does not pause to make sense of new words in reading. The student rarely uses tools such as the Bank of Powerful Language, the wordcatcher, and the word hunter role to collect interesting and powerful words.		The student seeks to make sense of new words in reading in a conscious manner. The student uses tools such as the Bank of Powerful Language, the wordcatcher, and the word hunter role to collect interesting and powerful words.
Word consciousness in writing • Sensory language • Metaphor/simile • Voice • Word choice • Variety • Expressiveness • Originality • Creativity	Writing lacks energy and evidence of personal engagement with the topic. Voice of the writer is unclear. Language is simple. Language devices such as metaphor and simile used only occasionally. Writing lacks originality.		Writing is full of energy and shows evidence of personal engagement with the topic. Ideas are presented with voice and style. Words are chosen for effect. Language devices such as metaphor and simile are carefully chosen and used in creative ways.
Academic language • Word consciousness • Accuracy	The student lacks awareness that instructions and information are given in precise language and makes little attempt to understand these. The student rarely uses academic language effectively in oral and written work.		The student is aware that instructions and information are given in precise language and attempts to understand these. The student uses academic language effectively in oral and written work.

USING A STUDENT RESPONSIBILITY RUBRIC

Another overall rubric focuses on work habits, behavior, and attitude (see below). The criteria were developed with the aid of our students at the beginning of the year. Every Friday, the students rate themselves on this rubric. At times, they also rate each other in their cooperative groups. These marks, collected over time, can be considered in assigning letter grades.

RUBRIC FOR STUDENT RESPONSIBILITY			
Dimensions of Student Responsibility	**Undeveloped—1** Listens to instructions and explanations with reminders. Often does not know what is being asked. Unwilling to participate in most tasks. Reluctantly helps others. Spends too much time socializing with peers. Demonstrates lack of motivation and inability to stay on task. Frequently turns in late assignments.	**2-3-4**	**Fully Developed—5** Listens intently to directions and explanations. Follows rules, routines, and procedures. Helps others without being asked. Is kind and supportive to classmates. Has a positive attitude. Exhibits high level of participation. Asks questions to clarify directions. Willingly tries new tasks in a confident manner. Works well with others and teacher. Is self-motivated. Turns in all assignments on time. Comes to class ready to work. Keeps planner up-to-date and uses it as an organizational tool without direction from teacher. Displays leadership skills. Assumes responsibility for being productive.

Thoughts to Ponder

Do not forget that the red marking pencil is the most lethal weapon a teacher possesses. Receiving a low mark with no understanding of why undermines a student's self-esteem and sense of self-efficacy.

Please remember that belief in your students and a caring heart go further toward change than any grade you could give. In the movie *Mr. Holland's Opus*, the music teacher, Mr. Holland, becomes quite frustrated with one of his struggling students. Exasperated, he declares, "Music is more than notes on the paper. Music must come from your heart!" Students trying to reach their writing potential need your help to do the best they can do on any given day. As a teacher, you are both a coach and a judge. We hope you can help them see that writing is more than just words on paper. Like teaching, writing must also come from the heart.

——— ❉ ———

Chapter 12

And Next . . .

This is the end, the conclusion, the finale of our journey together. We hope, however, that you see it as we see our work with students—as the beginning of your new journey as a word-conscious teacher. As you sail away, you are pointed in a worthwhile direction, with a good GPS system, aboard a sturdy vessel built with care and filled with lessons and ideas. We hope you are as excited by this new adventure as we are and that you find fellow sailors to share in your discoveries along the route. Hopefully, this book has provided enough scaffolding for you as a teacher to ensure a relatively smooth trip. We have discussed what to do and why to do it, and have presented models of how to do it in your classroom.

Teaching is never an easy job. It seems particularly troublesome in this age of government and district oversight. It seems that many forces are buffeting our ships along the way. Programs and guidelines often give us reading and writing activities that are isolated from each other and the rest of the curriculum. The standards, while important guideposts, often do the same. Teaching language arts in an integrated and focused manner when all of our students are at different places in their awareness of English language structures, in their ability to write cogently, and in their reading levels is daunting. As teachers, it is easy to become overwhelmed by the weight and frustration of this task. It is a struggle that all teachers, experienced and novice, face daily.

Our vision of an integrated literacy class where students dive deeply into discussions of children's literature and find their "writerly voice" through the use of powerful language can become a reality. In fact, we think it is imperative that it does. Students need reasons to learn vocabulary words. How many do you remember from the lists you studied when you went to school? Going to dictionaries to find word meanings is relatively useless (Miller & Gildea, 1987; Scott & Nagy, 2004). On the other hand, most people want to communicate their ideas clearly so that others understand what's inside their heads. Learning how to do that consistently, in school language, with precise word choice, is a talent worth cultivating. Connecting students' reading with their writing by focusing on the magic of language is grounded in both good theory and good practice.

Elements we know are important for learning and teaching are embedded in the program we've presented. We start with what the students bring to the class and build from there. We create a classroom environment where students work together to make meaning, where each is honored as both an individual and a collaborative member of the class, where we model and scaffold activities to bridge the independent work of students, and where we look beyond the classroom walls to published authors for models of effective language learning. We tickle the curiosity of students, push them to be creative, and provide strategies that go beyond a one-shot solution to a writing dilemma. Lucy Calkins (1994) said it well: "We need to give the writer something that will help not only today, with this piece of writing, but also tomorrow, with other pieces of writing . . . . If we can keep only one thing in mind—it is that we are teaching the writer and not the writing. Our decision must be guided by 'what might help this writer' rather than 'what might help this writing'" (p. 228).

Ultimately, we want to develop self-regulated learners who are excited by words and carry this enthusiasm into their everyday lives. In Bonnie's class one day, Andeep shared this response from his cousin in another city: "How did you learn to write like that!?" Apparently, he'd written a letter about a soccer game saying, "It was raining so hard it felt like shards of glass were piercing my shoulders." That's when we knew we'd achieved our goals. Here was a sixth-grade Punjabi boy writing, on his own, to tell his cousin about his life, using powerful language to do so. When Susie Cross's former students bounded toward her on the first day of school to show Gifts of Words they'd found over the summer, when Teresa Blackstone's students told her that their read-aloud book did not meet their expectations because the author didn't provide decent character descriptions, and when Bonnie's students told her that they finally understood what it means to be an author and to find a new way to enjoy reading, our suspicions were confirmed. These children had embraced word consciousness completely.

When we started this project, we recognized the lack of connection between what we knew to be good classroom practice and the materials available for teaching vocabulary. This problem still exists. One of the reasons for writing this book is to share how we were able to meld vocabulary learning with our set of beliefs and understandings. In particular, the development of word consciousness is a powerful tool for vocabulary learning that goes beyond teaching a prescribed set of words. It blends our knowledge of vocabulary learning and classroom practice so that students can read, use, and recognize words as tools of communication. We hope you take these ideas and develop them with your own twist and flair.

Bon voyage!

———✳———

References

Aitken, B., Haskings-Winner, J., & Mewhinney, R., et al. (2006). *Their stories, our history: Canada's early years.* Scarborough, Ontario: Thomson Nelson.

Allington, R. L. (2002). What I've learned about effective reading instruction from a decade of studying exemplary elementary classroom teachers. *Phi Delta Kappan, 83*(10), 740–747.

Anderson, R. C., Hiebert, E. H., Scott, J. A., & Wilkinson, I. A. G. (1985). *Becoming a nation of readers: The report of the Commission on Reading.* Champaign, IL: Center for the Study of Reading.

Anderson, R. C., & Nagy, W. E. (1992). The vocabulary conundrum. *American Educator, 16*(4), 14–18; 44–47.

Atwell, N. (1984). Writing and reading literature from the inside out. *Language Arts, 61*(3), 240–252.

_____. (1985). Writing and reading from the inside out. In J. Hansen, T. Newkirk, & D. Graves (Eds.), *Breaking ground: Teachers relate reading and writing in the elementary years* (pp. 147–165). Portsmouth, NH: Heinemann.

_____. (1987). *In the middle: Writing, reading and learning with adolescents.* Portsmouth, NH: Heinemann.

_____. (1998). *In the middle: New understandings about writing, reading, and learning.* (2nd ed.). Portsmouth, NH: Heinemann.

Au, K., & Mason, J. (1981). Social organizational factors in learning to read: The balance of rights hypothesis. *Reading Research Quarterly, 17*(1), 115–152.

Bakhtin, M. M. (1981). *The dialogic imagination: Four essays.* (M. Holquist, Ed.; C. Emerson & M. Holquist, Trans.). Austin: University of Texas Press.

Bare Books (2007). Franklin, WI: Treetop Publishing. http://www.barebooks.com.

Barton, B., & Booth, D. (2004). *Poetry goes to school.* Markham, Ontario: Pembroke Publishers.

Baumann, J. F., Kame'enui, E. J., & Ash, G. (2003). Research on vocabulary instruction: Voltaire redux. In J. Flood, D. Lapp, J. R. Squire, & J. Jensen (Eds.), *Handbook of research on teaching the English Language Arts* (2nd ed.; pp. 752–785). Mahwah, NJ: Lawrence Erlbaum.

Bear, D., Invernizzi, M., Templeton, S., & Johnston, F. (2000). *Words their way: Word study for phonics, vocabulary and spelling instruction.* Columbus, OH: Merrill/Prentice Hall.

Beck, I., & McKeown, M. (1991). Conditions of vocabulary acquisition. In R. Barr, M. Kamil, P. Mosenthal, & P. D. Pearson (Eds.), *Handbook of reading research: Vol. 2.* (pp. 789–814). New York: Longman.

Bellanca, J., & Fogarty, R. (1991). *Blueprints for thinking in the cooperative classroom.* (2nd ed.) Palatine, IL: RI/Skylight Publishing.

Blachowicz, C. (1987). Vocabulary instruction: What goes on in the classroom? *The Reading Teacher, 41*(2), 132–137.

Bloom, P. (2000). *How children learn the meanings of words.* Cambridge, MA: MIT Press.

Brownlie, F., & Close, S. (1992). *Beyond chalk and talk.* Markham, Ontario: Pembroke Publishers.

Butler, P. (2002). Imitation as freedom: (Re)forming student writing. *The Quarterly—National Writing Project, 24*(2). Retrieved April 10, 2007, from http://www.writingproject.org/cs/nwpp/print/nwp_docs/322.

Calkins, Lucy McCormick. (1986, 1994). *The art of teaching writing.* Portsmouth, NH: Heinemann.

Carey, S. (1978). The child as word learner. In M. Halle, J. Bresnan, & G. Miller (Eds.). *Linguistic theory and psychological reality* (pp. 264–293). Cambridge, MA: MIT Press.

Carroll, J. B., Davies, P., & Richman, B. (1971). *The American heritage word frequency book.* Boston: Houghton Mifflin.

Chafe, W., & Danielewicz, J. (1987). Properties of spoken and written language. In R. Horowitz & S. J. Samuels (Eds.), *Comprehending oral and written language* (pp. 83–113). San Diego, CA: Academic Press.

Chall, J., Jacobs, V., & Baldwin, L. (1990). *The reading crisis: Why poor children fall behind.* Cambridge, MA: Harvard University Press.

Christensen, L. (1998). Inviting student lives into the classroom: Where I'm from. *Rethinking Schools, 12*(52), 22–23.

_____. (2000). *Reading, writing, and rising up.* Milwaukee, WI: Rethinking Schools, Ltd.

Clark, C., Moss, P. A., Goering, S., Herter, R. J., Lamar, B., Leonard, D., et al. (1996). Collaboration as dialogue: Teachers and researchers engaged in conversation and professional development. *American Educational Research Journal, 33*(1), 193–231.

Clark, E. (1993). *The lexicon in acquisition.* Cambridge, U.K.: Cambridge University Press.

Close, S. (1988). The gift of words. *Prime Areas, 31*(1), 169–170.

Culham, R. (2003). *6+1 Traits of Writing.* New York: Scholastic Professional.

Cullinan, B. E., Scala, M. C., & Schroder, V. C. (1995). *Three voices: An invitation to poetry across the curriculum.* Portland, ME: Stenhouse.

Cummins, J. (2000). *Language, power, and pedagogy: Bilingual children in the crossfire.* North York, Ontario: Multilingual Matters.

Daniels, H. (1994). *Literature circles: Voice and choice in the student-centered classroom.* Portland, ME: Stenhouse.

_____. (2002). Expository text in literature circles. *Voices From the Middle, 9*(4), 7–14.

Elley, W. (1989). Vocabulary acquisition from listening to stories. *Reading Research Quarterly, 24*(2), 174–187.

Espy, W. R. (1975). *An almanac of words at play.* New York: Clarkson N. Potter.

Eyewitness Books. (2007). New York: DK Publishing. http://us.dk.com/static/cs/us/11/features/eyewitness.

Faulkner, W. (1968). Classroom statements at the University of Mississippi. In J. B. Meriwether & M. Millgate (Eds.), *Lion in the garden: Interviews with William Faulkner.* Lincoln, NE: University of Nebraska Press.

Graves, M. F., & Watts-Taffe, S. (2002). The place of word consciousness in a research-based vocabulary program. In A. Farstrup & S. J. Samuels (Eds.), *What research has to say about reading instruction* (3rd ed.; pp. 140–165). Newark, DE: International Reading Association.

Greenaway, T. (1994). *Jungle.* Eyewitness Books. London: Dorling Kindersley.

Harste, J., & Short, K., with Burke, C. (1988). *Creating classrooms for authors: The reading-writing connection.* Portsmouth, NH. Heinemann.

Hart, B., & Risley, T. (1995). *Meaningful differences in the everyday experiences of young American children.* Baltimore, MD: Brookes Publishing.

Hart, B., & Risley, T. (2003). The early catastrophe: The 30 million word gap by age 3. *American Educator, 27*(1). Retrieved October 29, 2007, from http://www.aft.org/pubs-reports/american_educator/spring2003/catastrophe.html.

Harvey, S. (1998). *Nonfiction matters: Reading, writing, and research in grades 3–8.* Portland, ME: Stenhouse.

Harvey, S., & Goudvis, A. (2000). *Strategies that work: Teaching comprehension to enhance understanding.* Portland, ME: Stenhouse.

Hayes, D. P., & Ahrens, M. (1988). Speaking and writing: Distinct patterns of word choice. *Journal of Memory and Language, 27,* 572–585.

Hayes, D. P., & Ahrens, M. (1988). Vocabulary simplification for children: A special case of "motherese." *Journal of Child Language, 15,* 401.

Heard, G. (1998). *Awakening the heart: Exploring poetry in elementary and middle school.* Portsmouth, NH: Heinemann.

Heath, S. B. (1983). *Ways with words: Language, life and work in communities and classrooms.* Cambridge, U.K.: Cambridge University Press.

Henry, S., Scott, J., Wells, J., Skobel, B., Jones, A., Cross, S., & Blackstone, T. (1999). Linking university and teacher communities: A "think tank" model of professional development. *Teacher Education and Special Education, 22*(4), 251–267.

Hirsch, E. D. (2003). Reading comprehension requires knowledge of words and the world. *American Educator, 27*(1), 10–13, 16–22, 28–29.

Kooy, M., & Wells, J. (1996). *Reader response logs.* Markham, Ontario: Pembroke Publishers.

Kriesberg, D.A., & Frederick, D. (1999). *A sense of place: Teaching children about the environment with picture books.* Englewood, CO: Teacher Ideas Press.

Lave, J., & Wenger, E. (1991). *Situated learning: Legitimate peripheral participation.* Cambridge, U.K.: Cambridge University Press.

Lindbergh, A. M. (1974). *Locked rooms and open doors: Diaries and letters of Anne Morrow Lindbergh, 1933–1935.* New York: Harcourt Brace Jovanovich.

Mikulecky, L. (1981). The mismatch between school training and job literacy demands. *Vocational Guidance Quarterly, 30*(2), 174–180.

Miller, G., & Gildea, P. (1987). How children learn words. *Scientific American, 257*(3), 94–99.

Moll, L. C., & Whitmore, K. F. (1993). Vygotsky in classroom practice: Moving from individual transmission to social transaction. In E. Forman, N. Minick, & C. Addison Stone (Eds.), *Contexts for learning: Sociocultural dynamics in children's development* (pp. 19–42). New York: Oxford.

Nagy, W., & Scott, J. (2000). Vocabulary processing. In M. Kamil, P. Mosenthal, P. D. Pearson, & R. Barr (Eds.), *Handbook of reading research, Vol. 3.* (pp. 269–284). Mahwah, NJ: Lawrence Erlbaum.

Nia, I. (1999). Units of study in the writing workshop. *Primary Voices K–6, 8*(1), 3–9.

Notable Trade Books for Young People. (May/June). Published annually by the National Council for the Social Studies in *Social Education.* http://www.socialstudies.org/resources/notable/.

Outstanding Science Trade Books for Students K–12. (March 2007). Published annually by the National Science Teachers Association in *Science and Children.* http://www.nsta.org/.

Pearson, P. D., & Gallagher, M. (1983). The instruction of reading comprehension. *Contemporary Educational Psychology, 8.*

Penno, J., Wilkinson, I. A. G., & Moore, D. W. (2002). Vocabulary acquisition from teacher explanation and repeated listening to stories: Do they overcome the Matthew effect? *Journal of Educational Psychology, 94*(1), 23–33.

Petersen, R. & Eeds, M. (1990). *Grand conversations.* New York: Scholastic.

Ray, K. W. (2006). Exploring inquiry as a teaching stance in the writing workshop. *Language Arts, 83*(3), 238–247.

Robb, L. (1994). *Nonfiction writing: From the inside out*. New York: Scholastic Professional.

Robbins, C., & Ehri, L. (1994). Reading storybooks to kindergartners helps them learn new vocabulary words. *Journal of Educational Psychology, 86*(1), 54–64.

Rosencrans, G. (1998). *The spelling book: Teaching children how to spell, not what to spell*. Newark, DE: International Reading Association.

Ruurs, M. (2000). *The power of poems: Teaching the joy of writing poetry*. Gainesville, FL: Maupin House.

Scott, J., & Nagy, W. E. (2004). Developing word consciousness. In J. Baumann & E. Kame'enui (Eds.), *Vocabulary instruction: Research to practice*. New York: Guilford Publications.

Scott, J. A., & Wells, J. (1998). Readers take responsibility: Literature circles and the growth of critical thinking. In K. Beers & B. Samuels (Eds.), *Into focus: Understanding and creating middle school readers* (pp. 177–197). Norwood, MA: Christopher-Gordon.

Short, K. G., & Burke, C. L. (1989). New potentials for teacher education: Teaching and learning as inquiry. *The Elementary School Journal, 90*(2), 193–205.

Sitton, R. (2002). *Sourcebook for teaching spelling and word skills*. Scottsdale, AZ: Egger Publishing.

Skobel, B. (1998). The gift of words: Helping students discover the magic of language. Unpublished master's thesis. Simon Fraser University, Burnaby, BC.

Stahl, S. (2003). How words are learned incrementally over multiple exposures: Implications for instruction. *American Educator, 27*(1), 18–19.

Stahl, S., & Nagy, W. (2006). *Teaching word meanings*. Mahwah, NJ: Lawrence Erlbaum.

Stickels, T. (2006). *The pocket book of frame games*. Beverly, MA: Fair Winds Press.

Swartz, L. (1993). *Classroom events through poetry*. Markham, Ontario: Pembroke Publishers.

Tharp, R. G., & Gallimore, R. (1989). *Rousing minds to life: Teaching and learning in social context*. Cambridge, U.K.: Cambridge University Press.

Vygotsky, L. S. (1978). *Mind in society*. (M. Cole, V. John-Steiner, S. Scribner, & E. Souberman, Eds.). Cambridge, MA: Harvard University Press.

Vygotsky, L. (1986). *Thought and language*. (A. Kozulin, Ed. and Trans.). Cambridge, MA: MIT Press.

Wells, J., & Reid, J. (2004). *Writing anchors: Explicit lessons that identify criteria, offer strategic support, and lead students to take ownership of their writing*. Markham, Ontario: Pembroke Publishers.

Wertsch, J. V., Tulviste, P., & Hagstrom, F. (1993). A sociocultural approach to agency. In E. Forman, N. Minick, & C. A. Stone (Eds.), *Contexts for learning: Sociocultural dynamics in children's development* (pp. 336–356). New York: Oxford University Press.

Wiggins, G., & McTighe, J. (1998). *Understanding by design*. Alexandria, VA: Association for Supervision and Curriculum Development.

Wingert, C., Crouse, D., Smith, J., Springer, T., Camacho, R., Fishburn, S., & Giauque, R. (2004). *The book book: Bringing book arts to scrapbooking*. Encino, CA: Autumn Leaves.

Zentella, A. C. (1997). *Growing up bilingual*. Malden, MA: Blackwell.

Bibliography
Books for Developing Word Consciousness

The following annotated bibliography of children's literature provides a starting point for the word-conscious teacher to begin creating a collection of favorite novels, picture books, and poetry. All the books cited in the text are referenced here, along with others we have used. We hope you will find many examples of the Gifts of Words in the work of all these wonderful writers.

NOVELS

Armstrong, Alan. *Whittington*. Random House, Yearling, 2006. Animals and children gather in a New England barn to listen to the stories of Dick Whittington, told by his namesake, a battered tomcat. The boy Ben is encouraged by the story to seek help in overcoming his dyslexia. Three story lines make this a gripping tale that has been compared to *Charlotte's Web*.

Armstrong, William H. *Sour Land*. New York: HarperCollins, 1971. Even the land seems to be against the Stone family when their mother dies, but when a new black teacher, Moses Waters, comes to the school, a friendship blossoms. The people of this sour land can't sit back and let a white family befriend a black man. There is no sugarcoated ending for this realistic story.

Babbitt, Natalie. *Tuck Everlasting*. Farrar, Straus and Giroux, 1975. When Winnie meets Tuck, she is confronted by an extraordinary decision.

_____. *Jack Plank Tells Tales*. Scholastic, 2007. A series of stories in which Jack looks for a suitable occupation only to realize that he is, of course, a storyteller.

Banks, Lynn Reid. *Tiger, Tiger*. Laurel-Leaf, 2007. This riveting historical novel compares the lives of two tiger cubs taken from their native jungle to ancient Rome. One, Brute, is trained to kill in the Colosseum, while the other, Boots, becomes the beloved pet of Caesar's daughter Aurelia.

Branford, Henrietta. *White Wolf*. Candlewick, 2007. Told from the perspective of a captive wolf who longs to be free, the book explores the relationships between trappers and the North American native people, and between people and animals.

Buffie, Margaret. *Who Is Frances Rain?* Kids Can Press, 1987. Lizzie is at the cottage and the family is bickering. In an abandoned cabin, she finds a pair of spectacles that take her back into the past. A ghost story, where the learning from the past affects the present.

Creech, Sharon. *Love That Dog*. Joanna Cotler Books, HarperTrophy, 2001. Inspired by a poem by Walter Dean Myers, this story shows one boy's journey toward an appreciation of poetry. See also *Walk Two Moons* (Joanna Cotler, 1994).

Curtis, Christopher Paul. *Bud, Not Buddy.* Delacorte Books, 1999. A 10-year-old boy in Depression-era Michigan sets out to find the man he believes to be his father.

Dahl, Roald. *Danny, the Champion of the World.* Puffin, 1975. A daring and hilarious fantasy about Danny and his dad in which Dahl uses language in scrumptious and unusual ways. See also *James and the Giant Peach, Charlie and the Chocolate Factory, The BFG,* and *The Fantastic Mr. Fox.*

DiCamillo, Kate. *Because of Winn-Dixie.* Candlewick Press, 2000. An enchanting story told in the voice of a lonely but resourceful protagonist with a charming canine companion.

_____. *The Tale of Despereaux: Being the Story of a Mouse, a Princess, Some Soup, and a Spool of Thread.* Candlewick Press, 2000. Winner of the Newbery Medal in 2004, this is a tale of hope, in which an assorted cast of characters obtain what seems at first to be beyond their reach. Magical storytelling.

Ellis, Deborah. *The Breadwinner.* Groundwood, 2000. Eleven-year-old Parvana lives in Kabul during Taliban rule. When her father is imprisoned, she disguises herself as a boy in order to work in the marketplace. See also *Parvana's Journey* (House of Anansi, 2002) and *Mud City* (House of Anansi, 2003), which complete the trilogy.

_____. *Jackal in the Garden: An Encounter with Bihzad.* Georgetown Publishers, 2007. This is the latest novel by this powerful writer.

Ellis, Sarah. *The Baby Project.* Groundwood, 1986. Jessie feels terrible after her baby sister dies in her crib. But as life returns to normal for her, she has guilty feelings. See also *Odd Man Out* (House of Anansi, 2006).

Fleischman, Paul. *The Half-a-Moon Inn.* Harper, 1980. Powerful language tells a fantastical tale of wicked highwaymen, evil innkeepers, and a brave boy.

Gardiner, John Reynolds. *Stone Fox.* Harper & Row, 1983. The story of Little Willie and the sled-dog race, in which Searchlight proves to be a dog in a million and Stone Fox makes a generous gesture.

Hiaasen, Carl. *Hoot.* Alfred Knopf, 2002. Offbeat and hilarious, this book is full of Hiaasen's trademark humor. Language used to great effect to describe characters.

Hoffman, Mary. *The Falconer's Knot.* Bloomsbury, 2007. Set in Renaissance Italy, this historical novel for young adults blends murder, romance, betrayal, and star-crossed lovers. Vivid historical details bring the setting to life.

Holm, Anne. *I Am David.* Methuen & Co., 1965. Having escaped from a concentration camp, David travels across Europe, silently and watchfully, avoiding involvement with anyone who shows interest in him. He gradually begins to gain hope and lose mistrust, finding his own identity in the process.

Horvath, Polly. *The Trolls.* Farrar, Straus and Giroux, 1999. A humorous book full of eccentric characters, it also deals with family relationships.

Hughes, Ted. *The Iron Man.* Faber, 1968. Written by one of the twentieth century's greatest poets, this story about a giant of iron who rises from the sea is evocative and entrancing.

Hunter, Erin. *Warriors: The New Prophecy. Book Two: Moonrise*. HarperTrophy, 2005. One in a series of fantasy books about clans of warrior cats.

James, P. D. *A Taste of Death*. Penguin, 1986. An adult mystery novel with twin murders in a London church.

Johnston, Julie. *Hero of Lesser Causes*. Lester Publishing, 1992. Twelve-year-old Keely tries desperately to help her brother Patrick, who is paralyzed by polio, which he contracted in the local pool. Set in 1946, this story defines the triumph of hope over self-pity.

Juster, Norton. *The Phantom Tollbooth*. Random House, 1961. This classic wears well, and is full of puns and plays on words.

Kogowa, Joy. *Naomi's Road*. Oxford, 1988. Set in the 1940s when Canada was at war with Japan, this story follows Naomi Nakane and her elder brother from Vancouver to an internment camp in the interior of British Columbia and then to a farm in Alberta.

Lawson, Julie. *White Jade Tiger*. Beach Holme, 1993. Jasmine's father goes to China, leaving her alone in Victoria. On a field trip to Chinatown, she mysteriously finds herself in the 1880s. Meeting a new friend, they travel to the Fraser Canyon searching for a white jade tiger, a magic amulet from ancient times. Three stories woven into one exciting novel.

Little, Jean. *Mama's Going to Buy You a Mockingbird*. Puffin, 1986. A sensitive novel dealing with bereavement, by a great Canadian writer.

London, Jack. *The Call of the Wild*. Tor Books, 1996. Originally published in 1903, this is a great adventure story. It begins, "Buck did not read the newspapers, or he would have known that trouble was brewing not alone for himself, but for every tide-water dog, strong of muscle and with warm, long hair, from Puget Sound to San Diego." What a great lead sentence!

Lowry, Lois. *The Giver*. Dell, 1993. Dark secrets underlie the perfection of Jonas's world. When he receives his assignment at age 12, he realizes he must undertake a seemingly impossible task. See also *Gathering Blue* and *The Messenger*.

_____. *Number the Stars*. Dell, 1990. During WWII, a 10-year-old Danish girl learns bravery as she hides a friend from the Nazis.

Magorian, Michelle. *Goodnight, Mr. Tom*. Harper Collins, 1981. A heartwarming story about a boy evacuated to the countryside during WWII. Billeted with Tom Oakley, Willie Beech begins to blossom. Not until the dark secret of his abuse at the hands of his mother is revealed can his healing begin.

MacLachlan, Patricia. *Sarah, Plain and Tall*. Harper & Row, 1985. The language of this contemporary classic reflects the tenderness and poignancy of the story. Sarah comes to look after Caleb and Anna and the family relationship gradually becomes permanent. Great for looking at setting and place.

Naidoo, Beverly. *Journey to Jo'Burg: A South African Story*. Harper, 1986. Mma lives and works in Johannesburg far away from her children. When the baby becomes sick, Naledi and Tiro set off on a journey to find her and bring her back.

O'Brien, Robert C. *Mrs. Frisby and the Rats of NIMH.* Heinemann, 1975. Mrs. Frisby has a sick child and is in dire straits, but she is aided by the extraordinary creatures, the rats of NIMH.

Oppel, Kenneth. *Silverwing.* HarperCollins Publishers Canada, 1998. The incredible adventures of a young bat named Shade. See also *Airborn* (2004); *Darkwing* (2007); *Skybreaker* (2007).

Park, Linda Sue. *A Single Shard.* Random House, 2001. Tree-ear, an orphan in Korea in the 1100s, lives hand to mouth and dreams of creating his own pots. Winner of the 2002 Newbery Medal.

Paterson, Katherine. *Bridge to Terabithia.* Harper & Row, 1977. One of the greatest writers for children, Katherine Paterson uses rich and melodious language. The friendship between Jess Aarons and Leslie Burke blossoms in the imaginary world they create together until a terrible tragedy shows Jess how much he has learned from Leslie. See also *The Great Gilly Hopkins* (Harper & Row, 1987); *Lyddie* (Puffin, 1991); *Rebels of the Heavenly Kingdom* (Puffin, 1983); *The Master Puppeteer* (Avon Camelot, 1981).

Paulsen, Gary. *Hatchet.* Puffin, 1988. A story of survival and courage and a book beloved by boy readers.

Pearce, Philippa. *Tom's Midnight Garden.* Dell, 1991. A classic well worth reading today—time travel was never so charming!

Pearson, Kit. *A Handful of Time.* Puffin, 1991. A time-travel story in which Patricia finds an old watch and discovers something of her mother's past and family history.

____. *The Sky Is Falling* (Viking Kestrel, 1989); *Looking at the Moon* (Viking, 1991); *The Lights Go on Again* (Viking, 1993). This realistic trilogy centers on the lives of Norah and her younger brother, Gavin, from the early days of the war in England through the experiences and adjustments of their five years as war guests in Canada.

Sachar, Louis. *Holes.* Douglas & McIntyre, 1998. The story of Stanley and his survival in juvenile detention, where the boys are forced to dig holes.

Rylant, Cynthia. *The Van Gogh Café.* Scholastic, 1995. Whimsical stories from a great writer.

Ryan, Pam Muñoz. *Esperanza Rising.* Scholastic, 2000. In the 1930s, a young Mexican girl falls from riches and becomes a migrant to California.

Smucker, Barbara. *Underground to Canada.* Puffin, 1977. Twelve-year-old Julilly is torn from her slave mother and moved to a plantation in the Deep South where she is cruelly treated. She and crippled Liza escape on the underground railway and travel to Canada and freedom.

Staples, Susan Fisher. *Shabanu, Daughter of the Wind.* Random House, 1989. Eleven-year-old Shabanu is facing an arranged marriage, but her parents fear she is too strong-willed to make a good wife. Sequel: *Haveli.*

White, E. B. *Charlotte's Web.* HarperCollins, 1974. Wilbur, Charlotte, and the other denizens of the barn star in this classic tale of love, loss, and friendship.

Yee, Paul. *The Bone Collector's Son.* Tradewind Books, 2004. Bing is a houseboy for a wealthy family in Chinatown. This is a ghost story from both Caucasian and Chinese perspectives, which gives insight into life in Vancouver in the early 1900s.

_____. *Curses of the Third Uncle*. James Lorimer, 1986. Fourteen-year-old Lilian is living in Vancouver in 1909 when her father mysteriously disappears. She can't trust her Third Uncle, and sets off on a dangerous journey to find her father.

_____. *Tales From Gold Mountain*. Douglas and McIntyre, 1989. The eight stories about Chinese immigrants to Canada range from ghost tales to romance, from China to northern gold fields and urban port towns.

Yolen, Jane. *The Devil's Arithmetic*. Puffin, 1990. Hannah is tired of hearing about family history. One Passover, she finds herself transported to a Jewish village in Poland in the 1940s. She will never again ask why she must remember—if she survives.

PICTURE BOOKS

Ackerman, Karen. *Song and Dance Man*. Alfred A. Knopf, 1988. A delightful story about a grandfather reenacting his days on the vaudeville stage for his grandchildren in the attic.

Ahlberg, Janet and Allan. *The Jolly Postman*. Little, Brown, 2001. An exploration of letter-writing in different voices and registers of language as fairy-tale characters receive their mail.

Alexander, Lloyd. *The King's Fountain*. Illustrated by Ezra Jack Keats. E. P. Dutton, 1989. A parable about a poor man who must change the king's mind when he plans to build a fountain that would deprive the city of water. Strong nouns and verbs.

Aliki. *Marianthe's Story: Painted Words, Spoken Memories*. Greenwillow Books, 1998. Marianthe's journey to a new life in the United States is told through her paintings and her storytelling in a classroom with a remarkably sensitive teacher. Lyrical language.

Andrews, Jan. *The Very Last First Time*. Illustrated by Ian Wallace. Groundwood, 1985. Eva Padlyat goes under the sea ice to collect mussels when the tide is out. Strong verbs paint a picture for the reader of Eva's experience.

Angelou, Maya. *Life Doesn't Frighten Me*. Edited by Sara Jane Boyers; illustrated by Jean-Michel Basquiat. Harry N. Abrams, 2002. Contemporary graffiti-style art is paired with Angelou's exuberant poem.

Bahr, Mary. *The Memory Box*. Albert Whitman, 1992. A poignant tale about preserving memories as Zach discovers his grandfather has Alzheimer's disease.

Base, Graeme. *Animalia*. Harry N. Abrams, 1986. Alliteration on every page as hidden objects and ideas illustrate the alphabet.

Baylor, Byrd. *Everybody Needs a Rock*. Aladdin Books, 1974. Poetic language and an interesting use of synonyms in building up an idea, that of ten rules for collecting rocks. See also *Guess Who My Favorite Person Is* (Aladdin Books, 1977) and *I'm in Charge of Celebrations* (Atheneum, 1986).

Blume, Judy. *The Pain and the Great One*. Dell Dragonfly Books, 1974. This family story about sibling rivalry is a good book for the memoir unit.

Bouchard, Dave. *If Sarah Will Take Me*. Orca Books, 1997. Poems and paintings show the strength of a man determined to make the most of life despite his disabilities.

_____. *If You're Not From the Prairie*. Simon & Schuster, 1995. Lyrical language paints a picture of the beauty of the prairie landscape.

Bridges, Shirin Yim. *Ruby's Wish*. Scholastic, 2002. The story of the author's grandmother and how she became one of the first women to go to college in China.

Brown, Margaret Wise. *The Important Book*. HarperTrophy, 1949. This pattern book uses language to describe everyday objects, beginning and ending with the important thing.

Brown, Ruth. *The Tale of the Monstrous Toad*. Andersen Press, 1996. Clever use of adjectives and strong verbs describe the monstrous toad that is too poisonous to be eaten by a monster.

Browne, Anthony. *My Dad*. Doubleday, 2000. Similes and idioms describe how a child feels about Dad.

Bunting, Eve. *Night of the Gargoyles*. Illustrated by David Wiesner. Clarion Books, 1994. When night comes the gargoyles creep on stubs of feet along the high ledges of a museum. Strong and unusual verbs are used to create atmosphere in this humorous and spooky book. Also by Eve Bunting: *Smoky Night* (Harcourt Children's Books, 1999); *Fly Away Home* (Clarion Books, 1993); *Riding the Tiger* (Clarion Books, 2001).

Cameron, Ann. *The Most Beautiful Place in the World*. Illustrated by Thomas B. Allen. Yearling, 1988. Juan, the little boy in the story, lives with his grandmother because his mother cannot care for him. A story of courage and resilience in Guatemala and an unforgettable introduction to the realities of life for children in developing countries.

_____. *The Stories Julian Tells*. Alfred Knopf, 1987. Family stories that feature a central character who is full of fun. See also *More Stories Julian Tells* and *Julian's Glorious Summer*.

Cooney, Barbara. *Miss Rumphius*. Viking, 1982. The "lupine lady" scatters seeds to make the world a more beautiful place. This is another book that can be used to study characterization.

Dorros, Arthur. *Abuela*. Dutton Children's Books, 2001. Rosalba is always going places with her grandmother, Abuela.

Duncan Edwards, Pamela. *Some Smug Slug*. Illustrated by Henry Cole. HarperCollins, 1996. An exploration of the art of alliteration as a slug slithers to an untimely end.

Elting, Mary, & Folsom, Michael. *Q is for Duck: An Alphabet Guessing Game*. Clarion Books, 1980. Q is for duck because a duck quacks. A great pattern book to provide a model for a class book.

English, Karen. *Nadia's Hands*. Boyds Mills Press, 1999. Nadia is a Pakistani-American girl who is nervous about being asked to be in her aunt's traditional Pakistani wedding.

Fanelli, Sara. *My Map Book*. HarperCollins, 1995. The book is a collection of maps, hand-drawn and labeled, showing real and imagined places. Included are maps of the author's family, her day, her tummy, and her school. Wonderful for stimulating personal writing.

Fleischman, Paul. *Weslandia*. Candlewick Press, 1999. Wesley's garden produces a crop of strange plants that help him to create an entire civilization, and in doing so, help him to make friends. Unusual nouns and verbs complement the unusual boy in the story.

Fox, Mem. *Wilfrid Gordon McDonald Partridge*. Penguin Books, 1984. A small boy tries to discover the meaning of the word *memory* so he can restore the memory of an elderly friend. See also *Shoes From Grandpa* (Orchard Books, 1989).

Heide, Florence Parry, & Gillian, Judith Heide. *The Day of Ahmed's Secret*. Illustrated by Ted Lewin. Lothrop Lee and Shepard Books, 1990. The language evokes the sights, sounds and colors of a busy day in Cairo. We hear and smell the city as well as see it.

Heller, Ruth. *Kites Sail High: A Book About Verbs*. Grosset & Dunlop, 1988. Verbs tell you something's being done, and this book demonstrates the role of the verb in a sentence. Colorful and attractive illustrations help the reader understand the text. Also by Ruth Heller: *Many Luscious Lollipops: A Book About Adjectives* (Grosset & Dunlop, 1989); *Merry-Go-Round: A Book About Nouns* (Scholastic Canada, 1990); *A Cache of Jewels and Other Collective Nouns* (Sagebrush Education Resources, 1998).

Henkes, Kevin. *Chrysanthemum*. HarperCollins, 1991. Chrysanthemum's enthusiasm about entering school is dampened when she is teased about her name. See also *Lilly's Purple Plastic Purse* (Greenwillow, 1996). Both stories have strong and interesting verbs, and the author shows rather than tells emotion. Also good for looking at characterization.

Hundal, Nancy. *I Heard My Mother Call My Name*. HarperCollins, 1990. A child lingers in the twilight, reluctant to go inside even though mother is calling. Lyrical, lovely language evokes time and place. See also *Prairie Summer* (Fitzhenry & Whiteside, 1999).

Khalsa, Dayal Kaur. *Tales of a Gambling Grandma*. Tundra Books, 1994. Grandma is a sharp card player!

Laden, Nina. *The Night I Followed the Dog*. Chronicle Books, 1994. Using rebus pictures, the author shows us the secret world of an amazing pet.

London, Jonathan. *Like Butter on Pancakes*. Illustrated by G. Brian Karas. Viking Kestrel, 1995. Metaphor and simile abound in this delightful account of a boy's day on a farm. See also *Condor's Egg* (1994/1999).

Lawson, Julie. *A Morning to Polish and Keep*. Red Deer Press, 1992. A family goes fishing in the early morning. The title indicates the lovely lyrical nature of the language.

Martin Jr., Bill, & Archambault, John. *Knots on a Counting Rope*. Henry Holt, 1987. Grandfather, who is blind, teaches his grandson the old ways.

McGugan, Jim. *Josepha: A Prairie Boy's Story*. Northern Lights Books for Children, Red Deer College Press, 1994. It's 1900, and an immigrant boy, unable to speak English, sits in the classroom with the younger children—"a blushing bull in primary row." His friendship with the narrator is described as Josepha leaves school forever to begin a lifetime of work on the prairie. Metaphor and simile are used as well as strong verbs and nouns.

Nobisso, Josephine. *Grandpa Loved*. Green Tiger Press, 1989. A young boy remembers his grandfather and the special times they had together.

Pinkwater, Daniel. *Aunt Lulu*. Macmillan, 1988. Aunt Lulu is a librarian who travels with her books by dog sled.

Polacco, Patricia. *The Keeping Quilt*. Simon & Schuster, 1988. A quilt is passed from generation to generation, symbolizing the love in a family. Other titles by Patricia Polacco that we use are *My Rotten Redheaded Older Brother* (Simon & Schuster, 1994); *Chicken Sunday* (Scholastic, 1992); *The Bee Tree* (Philomel Books, 1993); *Mrs. Katz and Tush* (Dell Publishing, 1992); *My Ol' Man* (Philomel Books, 1995); *Thank You, Mr. Falker* (Philomel Books, 1998).

Potter, Beatrix. *The Tale of Peter Rabbit*. F. Warne, 1902. Peter's father was put in a pie, and Peter nearly suffers the same fate.

Ringgold, Faith. *Tar Beach*. Crown Publishers, 1991. This book is based on the author's quilt painting of the same name. A family sits on the rooftop and dreams. A young girl imagines flying above her Harlem home, claiming all she sees for herself and her family.

Rylant, Cynthia. *The Relatives Came*. Aladdin Books, Macmillan, 1993. Cynthia Rylant's evocative prose celebrates family life. See also *When I Was Young in the Mountains* (E. P. Dutton, 1982).

Say, Allen. *Grandfather's Journey*. Houghton Mifflin, 1993. Grandfather goes from Japan to America but can't settle there, so he goes home again, but eventually returns to the United States. A true immigrant experience.

Scieszka, Jon, & Smith, Lane. *The True Story of the Three Little Pigs*. Viking Kestrel, 1989. The wolf was framed, and here he tells his true story.

Sheldon, Dyan. *The Whales' Song*. Red Fox, 1990. Lily's grandmother tells her that when she was young she used to leave gifts for the whales.

Smythe, Anne. *Islands*. Illustrated by Lazlo Gal. Groundwood Books, 1995. Laura and her mother walk through the snow across the frozen lake to an island. This is a lyrical evocation of a special place and the magic of a winter's day.

Spalding, Andrea. *Solomon's Tree*. Orca Books, 2002. A First Nations boy has a very special relationship with a tree. When it is blown down in a gale, his uncle carves a mask for Solomon that embodies the spirit of the tree. Language shows us, rather than telling, how dearly Solomon loves the tree.

Steig, William. *Brave Irene*. Farrar, Straus and Giroux, 1986. Steig is a masterful storyteller. His language introduces the reader to new and exciting words. Brave Irene is a wonderful character. See also *Amos and Boris* (Farrar, Straus and Giroux, 1971).

Stevenson, James. *When I Was Nine*. Greenwillow, 1986. A reminiscence of one special summer.

Trivizas, Eugene. *The Three Little Wolves and the Big Bad Pig*. Maxwell Macmillan International, 1993. A fractured fairy tale in which the pig is the bad guy.

Viorst, Judith. *The Tenth Good Thing About Barney*. Aladdin Books, Macmillan, 1971. In this classic book, a child is helped to understand the death of a pet.

Wiesner, David. *Flotsam*. Clarion Books, 2006. A wordless picture book with amazing imaginative pictures and great potential for storytelling. Also see *Tuesday* (Clarion, 1997).

Wild, Margaret. *Fox*. Kane-Miller, 2000. This powerful tale of friendship and betrayal between a fox and a magpie is set in the red-center of Australia. Strong language reflects the serious issues and deadly crisis at the heart of the story. Great characterization.

Yerxa, Leo. *Last Leaf, First Snowflake to Fall*. Groundwood, 1993. A dreamlike voyage into nature at the moment when fall turns into winter features lyrical words and beautiful collage illustrations.

Yolen, Jane. *Owl Moon*. Philomel Books, 1987. Father and child go owling one winter's night. Poetic language including simile and metaphor creates a sense of magic and mystery. We love the sense of setting and evocation of place.

POETRY

Alarcón, Francisco X. *Angels Ride Bikes*. Children's Book Press, 1999.

Berry, James. *When I Dance*. Puffin, 1988.

Booth, David. *'Til All the Stars Have Fallen: Canadian Poems for Children*. Illustrated by Kady MacDonald Denton. Kids Can Press, 1989.

Cassedy, Sylvia, Suetake, Kunihiro (trans.), & Bang, Molly (illust.). *Red Dragonfly on My Shoulder*. HarperCollins, 1992.

Dickinson, Emily. *Poetry for Young People*. Edited by Frances Schoonmaker Bolin. Sterling Publishers, 1994.

Fitch, Sheree. *If You Could Wear My Sneakers*. Illustrated by Darcia Labrosse. Doubleday, 1997.

Fleischman, Paul. *Joyful Noise: Poems for Two Voices*. HarperTrophy, 1988.

Grimes, Nikki. *Thanks a Million*. HarperCollins, 2006.

Hopkins, Lee Bennett. *Wonderful Words: Poems About Reading, Writing, Speaking, and Listening*. Illustrated by Karen Barbour. Simon & Schuster, 2004.

Hopkins, Lee Bennett. *Through Our Eyes: Poems and Pictures About Growing Up*. Scholastic, 1992.

Lee, Dennis. *Alligator Pie*. Macmillan of Canada, 1974.

Lesynski, Loris. *Dirty Dog Boogie*. Annick, 1999.

Merriam, Eve. *A Sky Full of Poems*. Yearling, 1986.

Nicholls, Judith. *Magic Mirror and Other Poems for Children*. Faber and Faber, 1985.

_____. *Midnight Forest and Other Poems*. Faber and Faber, 1987.

O'Neill, Mary. *Hailstones and Halibut Bones: Adventures in Colour*. Doubleday, 1961.

Paschen, Elise. (Ed.). *Poetry Speaks to Children*. Sourcebooks, 2005.

Plath, Sylvia. Mushrooms. In *Sylvia Plath: The Collected Poems*, edited by Ted Hughes. Buccaneer Books, 1981.

Prelutsky, Jack. (Ed.). *The Random House Book of Poetry for Children*. Random House, 1983.

Rampersad, A., & Roessel, D. (Eds.) *Poetry for Young People: Langston Hughes*. Scholastic, 2006.

Yolen, Jane. *Sea Watch*. Philomel, 1996.

INFORMATION BOOKS

Baylor, Byrd. *The Desert Is Theirs*. Tandem Library, 1987.

Denenberg, Barry. *The Journal of William Thomas Emerson: A Revolutionary War Patriot, Boston, Massachusetts, 1774*. Scholastic, 1998.

Gregory, Kristiana. *The Winter of Red Snow: The Revolutionary War Diary of Abigail Jane Stewart*. Scholastic, 1996.

McGovern, Ann. *The Secret Soldier: The Story of Deborah Sampson*. Scholastic, 1991.

Moss, Marissa. *Emma's Journal: The Story of a Colonial Girl*. Harcourt Trade, 2001.

Siebert, Diane. *Mojave*. HarperTrophy, 1988.

_____. *Heartland*. HarperTrophy, 1989.

Yolen, Jane, & Stemple, Heidi. *The Wolf Girls: An Unsolved Mystery from History*. Simon & Schuster, 2001.